That Place We Call Home

JOHN CREEDON

That Place We Call Home

A JOURNEY THROUGH the PLACE NAMES of IRELAND

Gill Books

Gill Books
Hume Avenue
Park West
Dublin 12
www.gillbooks.ie

Gill Books is an imprint of M.H. Gill and Co.

Permission to use lines from 'Ulster Names' by John Hewitt granted by
The John Hewitt Society.

978 07171 89854

Designed by Sarah McCoy
Illustrated by Ross Orr
Edited by Tara King
Copyedited by Neil Burkey
Proofread by Emma Dunne
Printed by CPI Group (UK) Ltd, Croydon, CRO 4YY

This book is typeset in Minion Pro.

*The paper used in this book comes from the wood pulp of managed forests.
For every tree felled, at least one tree is planted, thereby renewing natural
resources.*

A CIP catalogue record for this book is available from the
British Library.

5 4 3 2

ACKNOWLEDGEMENTS

This modest offering is not the definitive book of Irish place names. It is, however, born out of a love of place that was fostered by others.

I'd like to acknowledge the encouragement of my English teacher, Humphrey Twomey, and the other kind teachers I've had along the way. I'm indebted to the staff at UCC, in particular all at the Department of Folklore and Ethnology, for providing me with not just the key but an entire bunch of keys to help me unlock the stories within our beautiful *logainmneacha*.

Thanks to RTÉ, which has been my university campus for over thirty years, for its commitment to Ireland and not just the marketplace. Too many to name, I remember here colleagues who supported and encouraged me when I doubted myself. I toast the long days and the craic I shared with the remarkably talented team at RTÉ Cork. Here's to many more adventures. A huge debt of gratitude is due to our countless contributors, storytellers, listeners and viewers, without whom the work would stop.

I'd like to thank the Department of Culture, Heritage and the Gaeltacht, especially Dr. Pádraig Ó Cearbhaill, Chief Placenames Officer in the Placenames Branch. Similarly, I am grateful to Dr Frances Kane at the Northern Ireland Place Name Project; all at the National Archives for their invaluable work; Ordnance Survey Ireland for explaining the mechanics of map-making to me; *mo chairde ag* TG4; Cork City Library; the Heritage Council; and the National Museum of Ireland.

Thanks to Deirdre Nolan, Tara King, Aoibheann Molumby, Avril Cannon and Teresa Daly at Gill Books. I really appreciated the attention to detail and the kindness of the people at Gill.

Thanks to my parents Connie and Siobhán, and to all the old people who have gone before me. I am forever indebted for your legacy: a love of place that fills my heart. To my family and friends, thanks for the laughs and the love. To those who follow on behind, particularly my four daughters: Kate, Martha, Nanci and Meg; and to my grandchildren in Ireland, Australia and Scotland (Lucie, Mollie, Rosie, Ella, Bonnie, Cody and those not yet with us). I wish you love, happiness and a sense of home.

And to my soulmate, Mairéad, I'm forever grateful to you for your love and support. Here's to the open road and the bowl of Frosties!

CONTENTS

1

BACK TO BREAC

The names of a land show the heart of the race,
They move on the tongue like the lilt of a song.
You say the name and I see the place
Drumbo, Dungannon, Annalong.
'Ulster Names', John Hewitt

Thirty thousand feet over the Sahara on my way to Tanzania, I turn the page of my in-flight magazine and I'm startled as it reveals a full-page ad from Fáilte Ireland, with a green map of Ireland right at the centre. I'm ambushed by a somersault of the heart, as if it were a photograph of my own mother that had appeared without warning. That map, that place I call home, stares back at me like a familiar face in an unfamiliar crowd. That surge of recognition and connection fuels an ache to be reunited soon.

I'm not the first Irish person abroad, I suspect, to have had a lump in the throat, a knot in the gut or some other physiological reaction to an unexpected sighting of the map of Ireland, the green jersey or even the word Ireland. The very name itself is a thing of great beauty, and I look forward to sharing its evolution with you later in this book.

'The savage loves his native shore' is a universal principle, but when you add the Irish story of mass emigration, you'll better understand why that longing for home has deepened our love of place more than most. One Victorian visitor is said to have quipped that the Irish get homesick even when they *are* at home. Indeed, it's this love of place and language that sees Irish emigrant gatherings the world over belt out ballads that are often little more than lists of place names. Like a mantra, the repetition of these names keeps them alive in the heart of the emigrant and the generations of foreign-born Irish who have inherited this gene.

The place names of Ireland form more than a mere ballad; they create a symphony of names. Peel back the veneer of melody and the meanings of the place names are revealed. Within them lie the clues to understanding the nature of the land of Éireann and the people who walked this stage before us. 'The Land of Robins', 'Patrick's Bed', 'The Eagle's Nest', 'The Valley of the Mad' are surely a call to investigate. From boyhood, Ireland's place and field names, and the stories they reveal, have provided nutrition for both mind and soul, as I tramped across the fields to gather home my uncle's cows with only a collie for company. These days my area of discovery has widened. As I travel the highways, byways and boreens of Ireland, the old Irish phrase *ar bóithrín na smaointe* returns to me, capturing the mood perfectly. It means 'daydreaming', or literally, 'on the little bye-roads of thought'.

The subject itself is truly a magnificent one, and certainly one in which you won't regret becoming absorbed. The one thing I would advise when it comes to place names is not to be put off by the Irish language element. It's all about cracking the code, and that code is actually quite simple once you understand a handful of the most commonly used terms, like 'Cnoc/Knock/Mountain' and 'Lios/Lis/Fort'. Some of the words you probably already know but don't realise it. So give yourself credit. You're a Gaelic scholar in a cocoon! I trust you will learn more from this book, but if all you know at this point is 'Baile/Bally/Town' and 'Mór/More/Big', then you're already off to a great start. Welcome to Big Town!

BOHERBOY, COUNTY CORK
Boherboy – An Bóthar Buí
Bóthar – Road
Buí – Yellow
Boherboy therefore means 'the yellow road'.

I've had a sort of on-again/off-again/on-again relationship with my native language. As a boy, I went through the primary school years speaking Irish at An Mhainistir Thuaidh (the North Monastery), a huge Christian Brothers campus with primary, secondary and technical schools on site. It catered for over two thousand boys on the predominantly working-class slopes of Cork City's northside.

I was the youngest of 51 boys in my class, so little surprise that I struggled in most subjects, except *amhránaíocht* ('singing class'). I entered the North Monastery as a six-year-old, just as the country prepared to mark the 50th anniversary of the Easter Rising of 1916. Boyish patriotism surged through my veins as we marched around the schoolyard in perfect time, belting out battle cries like 'Óró sé do bheatha 'bhaile' and planning how I could die for Ireland without my mother knowing.

However, whatever about the past tyranny of the British, the daily school-room injustices slowly eroded my love for this nationalist dream, and with it went my desire to die for Ireland. Instead, I found myself longing to live; to live like George Best, to kiss girls and to drink champagne in nightclubs and do all the other things that were only allowed in the English language!

The late teenage years were spent with my back defiantly turned to conservatism, the Catholic Church, the GAA, the Irish language and to all who claimed copyright over Irishness. I rejected De Valera's 'comely maidens' for 'foreign wans', Spanish students and tourists who might bring a little spice into a very bland life. Once I completed my Leaving Cert Irish paper, I put the pen down and it was a full stop. The Irish speaker inside of me was silenced for two decades. Instead, I enrolled in UCC to study English and Philosophy. Granted, I did more talking about them than studying them, but I suppose you can get away with that when English and Philosophy are your subjects of choice.

As Thatcher's Britain thrashed the poor of the country, I witnessed nightly the English and Welsh miners cudgelled by their own police. I began to question the notion that any outside culture was automatically better than the Irish misery I had inherited. With the passing of the years and, more significantly, the passing of my beloved mother, I began to recall again the caress of 'the old people'. Like when Mrs Buckley would welcome me: 'Wisha, *tar isteach* out of the rain, *a leanna*! You're getting as big as a *buachallán buí*.' Yes, being compared to a giant ragwort was a term of endearment for a growing boy.

Having put years of distance between myself and the shackles of those who wished to 'beat a bit of Irish art and culture' into me, I now found myself being drawn to those who simply lived it, people who were still connected, unknowingly, to the old ways. Trips from my new life in Dublin back to the Muskerry Gaeltacht sparked a curiosity and a deep sense of a journey home within me. My father, in the passenger seat, would point out some sloping field where he once played a match against Dromtarriff in 1931, saying, 'By God, they were tough *buachaillí* from Drom Tairbh ... and sure why wouldn't they, and they from the hill of the bull! They could run as fast uphill as they could downhill. I s'pose being chased by a bull could do that to you alright,' he'd laugh. 'And that's Annahalla Bridge over there! Abhainn na hEala, the river of swans. Cáit a' Phéist used to live away over that way. The old people used to say she could cure any ailment with some oul' worm she had.' (I've since been told that Cáit's nickname referred to the leech she used for bloodletting.)

I was drunk on the nectar of his words. I couldn't get enough. Trips to West Kerry and to Inis Oírr and Connemara followed, where I marvelled at how unusual the Irish language sounded when spoken in the different dialects, each unique to its own region. Even within a region, areas would have an identifiable *canúint*, or accent. Now there's another great Irish word, *canúint*, taken from the Irish word *canadh*, meaning 'singing'. Yes, that's it exactly! Your *canúint* is the melody in your accent.

Twenty years after I left UCC, I went back to my alma mater, and this time I was serious. I took a two-year diploma course in Regional Studies. This godsend drew on the remarkable riches of the Folklore, History and Archaeology departments at the university. For the first time in my life, I was the first student into class and the last one out, every time, and my homework was done without fail!

Our lecturers took us on field trips beneath the footpaths of my beloved Cork City, to where St Finbarr first knelt to pray, to the alleyways of the old city where Vikings added Old Norse to the local vocabulary, and where French and Breton was later spoken. Is this when the citizens of Cork first began to develop their sing-song *canúint*? Or did that come later, with the arrival of the Welsh Fusiliers? My God, these people were real. They lived and loved and lost and longed for the same things as me. The Cork merchant princes with their pointy-toed buckled shoes strode around these very same streets. Streets they named after themselves. It never fails to amaze me.

I grew up around the corner from St Patrick's Bridge in Cork. Think for a moment of the historical giants that crossed that very bridge. In 1963 we had President John F. Kennedy, in 1849, Queen Victoria of England, and in 1858, Charles Dickens. I can see Christy Ring at the front of a lorry raising the Liam MacCarthy Cup to the thousands lining the route to see our heroes cross the Lee as All

Ireland champions. Michael Collins would have swaggered along its footpath, and of course jazz legend Ella Fitzgerald probably sashayed across the bridge as she was accompanied from the Cork Opera House to her hotel on MacCurtain Street at the 1980 Jazz Festival. Any time I walk over it, that's the realisation that hits me: the history that's imprinted in the ground beneath my feet, and all the dramas that must have been played out half an inch below the spot I now occupy. When you stop and think about it, when you take it all in, it's enough to put the worries of your own life into perspective, and that's what I absolutely love about these investigations.

As a boy, I would wonder what might be *in* the mud beneath St Patrick's Bridge. Was a sword or two thrown in there following a street battle? Have engagement rings or even wedding rings been hurled in there during heated rows of a Saturday night? You can picture someone shouting, 'You can take your @*!&@ engagement ring and shove it, ya langer!'

Are there murder weapons or skeletons lying in the many layers of the riverbed? Whatever the case, you can bet your life there's a few interesting finds down there. Consider for a moment the feet that have crossed Dublin's O'Connell Bridge and what lies beneath it, or indeed beneath the footpaths and fields of your locality.

What really draws me in, however, are the clues left by our ancestors – signposts that point us towards who our predecessors were, how they lived and how they made sense of this very same world that we now inhabit. The wonderful thing is that many of these signposts are just that, actual signposts! I have criss-crossed Ireland a thousand times, and every time I do, I feel our ancestors are speaking to us through the place names written on the signposts of Ireland. It's like they are trying to tell us something.

My lifelong *grá* for place names, and languages too for that matter, without doubt came from my father, Connie Creedon. A good-humoured man, he split his time between being a bus driver, a newsagent and a father to 12 children. My dad spoke beautiful

Irish, as well as classical Greek, Latin and, of course, English. He adored words. You couldn't engage him in conversation without him throwing in a few lines of Homer's *Odyssey*, a quote from Shakespeare, an epic love poem by Máire Bhuí Ní Laoghaire or even a line or two from comic-book hero Desperate Dan in *The Dandy*, whom he loved. A simple request for the admission price to the pictures might elicit a quote from *Gone with the Wind*, before he handed over the few coins with a wink.

I remember when I was around seven or eight years of age, I was bragging about a goal I had somehow managed to score in a school hurling match. Humouring me, my father sat back and listened. As soon as I was done recollecting my on-pitch heroics, he teasingly remarked, 'Well, John Joseph. Methinks you're suffering from elephantitis of the cranium.'

I looked at him.

'Do you know what that means?' he asked.

'I don't, Dad. What does it mean?'

'Ah, you'll have to think about it,' came the response.

I thought about it for a bit and sure enough the penny eventually dropped. Hadn't he just informed me that my malady was little more than a swelled head.

The roots of my father's love for the Irish language could be found in his homeplace of Inchigeelagh in the parish of Uibh Laoghaire, meaning Land of the O'Learys. He always referred to the village of Inchigeelagh as a *breac Gaeltacht*, a term inspired by that brilliant Irish word *breac*, meaning 'speckled'. It features in the phrase *breacadh an lae*, which means 'the speckling of day, i.e. daybreak, and of course in the term for the Halloween classic *bairín breac*, which means 'speckled cake'. *Breac* also means 'trout', on account of that fish's speckled skin. Anyway, Inchigeelagh, which sits beautifully on the eastern shore of Lough Allua, was referred to as a *breac Gaeltacht* because it was essentially speckled with Irish-speaking households, while English was spoken in others. Both languages, however, were in daily use at the counter of my grandmother's post office in the village. I expect it was while sitting on a raised chair behind the counter and beside his loving mother that Connie Creedon the little boy absorbed so much in two languages.

My mother, Siobhán, however, was quietly spoken and thoughtful. One of 10 girls, she grew up in an English-speaking home in Adrigole, overlooking Bantry Bay, out on the beautiful Beara Peninsula. Although a small farmer, her father, William Blake, shared his name with the English poet, underlining my mother's paternal roots as English Protestant, or perhaps Norman (from the De Blaca family who came over with Strongbow). Either way, despite their humble circumstances, my mother developed beautiful handwriting and a leaning towards the arts.

As a little boy, I was incredibly lucky to have had the best of two worlds. We lived in the heart of the city, which pulsed to the clippity-clop rhythm of the giant Shire draught horses of Murphy's brewery beside us. The melody was provided by the singalong accent of the citizens and the cacophony of Creedons that buzzed day and night beneath our roof. In complete contrast, long summer days back west seemed to stretch out in spacious meadows filled with the sweet smell of hay and honeysuckle. Less time for talk and more for daydreaming.

Due to the fact that my parents worked such long days raising 12 children and maintaining a shop with 6am to 1.30am opening hours, family trips back west were last-minute, and involved loading the car with as many of us as the car could take. It's often assumed that scenery is wasted on the young, but we genuinely 'got it'; we saw the beauty of these places. We could feel my mother's excitement spread through the car as the road narrowed and the fine flat farms on the western side of Cork City gave way to bog and bulrush, *sceach*, *sliabh* and storytelling.

'Will we go through Inchigeelagh or head straight for "the Bantry Line", Siobhán?'

'Yerra, we'll go through Inchigeelagh so, Connie, but we won't delay while we still have the bit of daylight.'

As we arrive in the village, my father points out Johnny Timmy Johnny's hardware and grocery shop. It's made entirely of corrugated iron from walls to barrel-top roof, and it straddles the river with just a gable end perched on either bank.

'I remember Johnny's father, Timmy Johnny. And by God, was he precise! Back during "the emergency", when things were scarce, I saw him, with my own two eyes, cut a raisin in half to make up the exact weight. What do ye make of that? He was an honest man. He would never "do" you, but by Christ he wouldn't go over either. He was a brilliant man.'

Our 14 first cousins ran the mill, post office and family hotel in Inchigeelagh, and a cluster of them would be out in a flash for frantic conversations through the car window. Uncle John was behind, larger than life and reaching in the window to hug and kiss his baby brother Con.

'Who's that in the back? Is it yourself, Geraldine? By God, there's my namesake – John Joseph – and all the other lovely girls and boys. Will ye come in for one quick cup of tea?'

'Oh Lord no, John, we have to belt for Adrigole. Kit will have the table laid.'

And with that we are gone.

With my little nose pressed against the rear passenger window, I peer out as the car gains momentum. Hedgerows laden with fuchsia, montbretia, wild roses and honeysuckle blur into an impressionist splash of reds, greens, lemon and vivid orange. The breathtaking scenery around *mo áit dhúchais*, meaning 'the place of my heritage', is celebrated in the beauty of its place names. We would first pass through Ballingeary/Béal Átha an Ghaorthaidh, meaning 'ford of the river that flows through woods', then head on for the Pass of Keimaneigh/Céim an Fhia, meaning 'leap of the deer', and on to Kealkill/An Chaol Choill, meaning 'the narrow wood', before emerging at Bantry/Beanntraí, meaning 'kingdom of the chieftain Beannt'. After leaving Bantry, it was a climb and descent into Glengarriff/An Gleann Garbh, meaning 'the rough glen', with its almost subtropical microclimate, after which we would then drive by the Victorian grandeur of the Eccles Hotel, with its wrought-iron veranda and palm trees.

The roads back then were nothing like what they are today, so allowing for puncture repairs, cattle gridlock at milking time and sheep acting the goat, the 150km journey from the city centre out to Allihies/Na hAilichí, meaning 'the cliff fields', at the western edge of the Beara Peninsula, could take you around three hours. Needless to say, there was plenty of time for storytelling, and behind every place name lay a story. Take, for example, Céim an Fhia, which again means 'leap of the deer'. I suspect it could also be translated as the 'path of the deer'. Anyway, during one of our drives out west, my father told me the story behind its name. Apparently, one day a beautiful stag was being hunted by a wealthy British redcoat on horseback. When it reached the cliff edge, the stag backed up and made one huge leap across this ravine in an attempt to escape his hunter. The chasm is about 50 yards wide, so I don't know just how much truth there is to this story; perhaps it wasn't quite as wide before the paved road went in, or perhaps some details in the story have changed with the passage of time, but, to be honest, it doesn't matter. That story has stuck with me all these years, and any time I drive through the Pass of Keimaneigh, the boy within is on the lookout for a huge stag on the clifftop, or a redcoat ambush on the road.

On the way to Céim an Fhia, you pass a townland called Tír na Spideoige. This has always been a favourite of mine. The word *tír* is Irish for 'land' or 'countryside', while *spideog* is the Irish for 'robin redbreast'. So Tír na Spideoige simply translates as 'the land of the robins', which wouldn't sound out of place in a Brothers Grimm fairy tale when you think about it. Beyond the beauty of the name, it underlines the nature of the people who walked this land. If the name 'land of the robins' denotes ownership, then clearly the people were acknowledging nature's dominion over this land, and their own footprint therefore would be light.

There's action and adventure in the place names around here too. Apart from the aforementioned stag hunt, the name Inchigeelagh (Inse Geimhleach, meaning 'island or river strand of the hostages') raises the question, 'What hostages?' There are many suggested answers, but given that the place name existed long before the persecution of the native Irish by Cromwell's forces, it can't be that. My own theory is that Viking raids up the River Lee may have caused locals to hide on the *crannóg* out on the lake. A *crannóg* is a man-made island with a hidden causeway just beneath the lake's surface, so the path to safety was familiar only to locals. I can see my ancestors gathering up their prized possessions and running for the safety of the lake, to wait silently without as much as snapping a twig until they felt it safe to carefully emerge to survey the damage.

However, my research has since informed me that the *crannóg* near Inchigeelagh has had a variety of names, including 'Mehigan's Island', and dates from long before early medieval times, when chieftains would have used it to hold hostages from neighbouring clans. Aha! My question has finally found its answer.

- -
BALLINCOLLIG, COUNTY CORK
Ballincollig – Baile an Chollaigh
Baile – town/homeplace
An Chollaigh – Collach (from the surname Coll)
Ballincollig therefore means 'the town of An Collach'.

One summer's evening in Inchigeelagh, after a day spent diving into the River Lee at a stretch known locally as 'the island', I remember my cousin Willie John pointing out the road that led to Poulanargid, which in Irish is Poll an Airgid, meaning 'the hole of the money'.

'Is the money still there?' I asked eagerly.

'Doubt it. I'd say 'twas gold and chalices and stuff, hidden by the monks long ago.'

'Will we get a couple of shovels and try anyway?'

'Erra, no. 'Tis too far and sure they say it's all gone anyway. I'd say the Black and Tans took it.'

Some claim that Poulanargid actually means 'the silver hole', a reference to the stream that flows there. Perhaps it does, but I'd still get the shovel ready if I were allowed.

Many of the *logainmneacha* ('place names') are prehistoric and were given in languages that are now obsolete, so their meanings are lost to us. Others have survived, like Lough Allua (Locha Lua), meaning 'the lake of the Lee', although it's also been suggested that it's named after Lugh/Lú, the old pre-Christian figure who also gave his name to County Louth/Contae Lú.

Lough Allua forms part of the Lee river system. It's a fine big lake, about a mile wide and three miles long (six by road). It's bounded by two villages: Ballingeary at its western end, where the River Lee enters the lake, as if to take a rest, before it emerges at Inchigeelagh, on its most easterly shore. Here, the lake narrows and reverts to river form, the Lee gathering pace yet again on its journey towards Cork City and out to sea.

The landscape around Uibh Laoghaire is a hunter's paradise. As evidenced by the place names, it's full of forest and fen, with lashings of fresh water. River, stream, lake and bracken provide the perfect cover for wildlife. Deer, rabbit, woodcock and all forms of game once drew in the Victorian visitors that sustained the family hotels in the nearby villages: Cronin's Hotel at Gougán and the Eccles Hotel beyond in Glengarriff. Each hotel was a handy coach-ride away from the next. There were boats for hire on the lake that splashed to the sound of salmon, trout and pike. Lough Allua was the jewel in this crown.

My mother's countryside, 40 miles further west, provides a beauty of massive contrast. Here, the rugged Caha Mountains sweep down to meet the mighty Atlantic Ocean; it is a far more dramatic scene than the soft landscape of fern and gentle waters of my dad's *áit dhúchais*.

On the journey west, my father would tease my mother about which homeplace was the better of the two. It was hard to out-play a hand that boasted an ocean, a milder climate and the mighty Hungry Hill, so my dad would always hold his best card for last: Lough Allua, the king of lakes.

While Adrigole has some notable lakes itself, none could trump Allua, and Dad would play that card with perfect timing. The only lake visible from the road as you approach Adrigole is Loch Mór ('big lake'). In truth, it's the size of a small field, but all things are relative, and if it's the biggest pond in the immediate vicinity then an ancient man without a bus pass is perfectly entitled to call it big. However, a bus driver with a few miles on the clock (like my dad) who swaggers into the parish could be forgiven for seeing the funny side of it.

Dad would wait until the spot emerged on the horizon. Then, like clockwork, he would say, 'Right, boys and girls! Wait now till you see the size of this lake. Loch Mór, it's called! Wait and you'll see it any second now. Keep watching! Keep watching! QUICKLY, LOOK! THERE! That's it, gone now!'

My mother would teasingly scold him, 'Connie, would you stop!'

Of course, Dad wouldn't pay any heed to this, preferring instead to milk the devilment for all he could.

'We'll have to go fishing there some day, lads,' he'd smile. 'I'd say there's some right monsters in there altogether!'

The lesson to be learned here is context. Just because a feature might be called 'the big hill', it doesn't necessarily mean it's some gargantuan landmark, but rather that it's the biggest in that particular area.

CLONAKILTY, COUNTY CORK
Clonakilty – Cloich na Coillte
Cloich – Stone/Stone building
Na Coillte – Woods
Clonakilty therefore means 'the stone in the woods'.

Context is one of the many filters I apply when deciphering a place name. Not only have our place names been altered through transliteration by the British, but words themselves are organic; their meanings change.

For example, my Aunt Eileen ran a small shop in Dungarvan called Cúil na Gabhair Dairy. Like most of us, I learned that the word *cúl* means 'back', as in *an cúl chlós* ('the backyard'), *cúl an tí* ('the back of the house') or *an cúl doras* ('the back door'). In which case, 'Cúil na Gabhair' could mean 'the goat's rear', or even 'the goat's backside'. Excuse me! My aunt Eileen would never print such a term over her shop. When I enquired, her son Ben explained that the Irish term *cúil* doesn't literally mean 'the back', but rather 'the part we cannot see from here'. So Cúil na Gabhair points to the side of the hill (a nook or recess) where the goats hang out. This would also suggest that the popular house name Cool na Greine (Cúil na Gréine) means 'sunny side' or 'suntrap' and not 'the back of the sun'.

There are many more examples where an Irish word does not quite match its English translation, *fear gorm* being an obvious example. It means 'black man' but translates literally as 'blue man'. Methinks the Irish word *gorm* was a far more subtle shade than plain old blue. Or else it may have been a reference to the indigo headgear and sails of the North African visitors to our Western shores. Furthermore, the term *fear dubh* (literally, 'black man') was already taken – it meant the devil!

There's a little manoeuvrability with most words, and the same is true with place names. A word or term we use today may have meant something slightly different a long time ago. Don't be put off by this. On the contrary, in all my years of exploring the subject, I have found ambiguity the perfect opportunity for a thousand conversations with men in tractors and place-name debates in village pubs. It certainly beats just learning it off by heart from a book!

- -

YOUGHAL, COUNTY CORK
Youghal – Eochaill
Eochaill – Yew Wood
This translation tells us that Youghal had a yew-wood forest at one point. Interestingly, in 2019, one of that year's many raging storms resulted in high tides on Youghal's Claycastle Beach exposing remnants of an ancient forest floor, subsequently nicknamed the 'drowned forest'.

Ptolemy's map of Ireland, the first of its kind, was created around 140 AD, but place names existed long before maps or signposts. Picture the scene a thousand years before Ptolemy's map. Some ancient Celt wishes to purchase cattle from another farmer. Clearly, they will have to arrange a time and place for the transaction.

'I'll see you tomorrow at sunrise.'

'Grand job. Where?'

'Do you know that big black rock? The one down by the river?'

'I do. Perfect. See you then.'

And so, a place called Blackrock (An Charraig Dhubh) is born.

Remember when you were a small child and there was always the danger that if you went rambling you might get lost? Or if a place was crowded and you lost sight of your parents, you might never ever find your way home? Well, for our ancestors, landmarks and place names formed the map of the mind. Without them, even an adult could get lost. These were verbally handed down through the generations. The Irish term for folklore is *béaloideas*, from the words *béal*, meaning 'mouth', and *oideas*, meaning 'instruction', so place names and family trees were passed from generation to generation by word of mouth. Furthermore, the study of 'the lore of notable places' was a subject in its own right, known as *Dindsenchas*. The modern Irish word for the study of topography is *dinnseanchas*. More about that ancient art later, however.

Most of Ireland's place names were settled over two thousand years ago and, as illustrated above, they mainly concerned themselves with immoveable features on the landscape. Examples that spring to mind would include Knockmore/An Cnoc Mór, meaning 'the big mountain', or Kinsale/Cionn tSáile, meaning 'the headland of the sea'. Interestingly, Cionn tSáile was transliterated as 'Kinsealy' in North County Dublin. As the once-nomadic Celts settled, man-made features began to appear on the land, and, for the first time, in the place names too. Hence, we saw names emerge like Carrigadrohid/Carraig an Droichid, meaning 'the bridge by the rock', or Donegal/Dún na nGall, meaning 'the fort of the foreigners', and so on.

Just as an archaeologist will trace the evolution of people from the lowest stratum to the surface, we will dig down and unearth the story of Ireland through its place names, from the first settlers who stood in awe at the beauty of their discovery to the time of St Patrick and the spread of Christianity. We will witness the development of our towns and cities from monastic settlements, and feel the imprint of the Viking raider and Norman invader on the land. We will hear the sound of our place names change as the plantation of Ireland by the English is reflected in the names given to vast estates and their adjoining villages. We will hear the cry of the poor captured in place names like Baile na mBocht, and view religious persecution remembered at Carraig an Aifrinn, the rock altar where mass was celebrated in the wind and rain on pain of death. We will also hear the trumpet reveille of the Gaelic Revival as it awakened a new interest in our noble past and a thirst for freedom. We will consider the ostentatious brag inherent in the names of many Celtic Tiger housing estates, and perhaps, in our lifetime, we will witness a new age of post-pandemic enquiry from those of us who stand on Ireland's stage today. You can tell your grandchildren you were part of it.

2

IN THE BEGINNING WAS THE
WORD ... AND IT WAS SPOKEN!

Places had names long before they were written down. We had committed place names to memory long before we had maps, just as we had memorised stories before we had books. The spoken word predates the written word, and the people of this island have proven themselves adept at both. All knowledge worth remembering had to be memorised, as people could neither read nor write. Reference books hadn't been invented – indeed books themselves hadn't been invented – so medicinal cures, recipes, law, history, geography and family trees all had to be committed to memory and carried around in someone's head. Can you imagine a world with no census, no birth certs, no written records? In this day and age where there is an everlasting record of everything, the very idea of it seems almost too surreal to fathom.

At night, people would gather round the fire as the storyteller began weaving a tapestry of tales. These sessions would usually open with the line 'fadó, fadó' ('long, long ago'), the Irish equivalent of 'once upon a time'. To keep the listener's attention, the tale was woven with epic battles, dire warnings, giant serpents and struggles between good and evil. Through this tapestry, a variety of moral values and 'the story of us' was passed along to eager ears.

How one head could hold so much crucial information must have been a source of awe to the ancient Irish, who placed the druids and bards as second only to royalty in Irish society. There was a strict pecking order in the bardic tradition, and it took years to master the craft of *na filí* (the great Gaelic poets). There were seven levels to the trade. The lowest level was that of *bard*, rising all the way to *ollamh*. To attain this lofty title, a *bard* had to study for at least 12 years, mastering 250 primary stories, 100 secondary stories and 300 complicated verses along the way. Interesting that the word *ollamh* is still in use in Irish universities to denote a professor.

Fleadh Cheoil na hÉireann, the traditional Irish music festival, also reserves the honorary title Ard Ollamh for someone who has made an outstanding contribution to traditional music. Indeed, the Irish music tradition itself has been built on a foundation stone of learning tunes by ear. Memorising through repetition has seen tunes take on the personality and grace notes of the local master. Sometimes the subtle nuance of a place will permeate the music. 'Sligo style' comes not from a book, but from listening and repeating over and over again. Musicians talk of 'handing down' the music to the next generation.

On one occasion, I remember savouring the music of Sliabh Luachra. Now there's a place name to contend with. It translates as 'hill of rushes', for that's exactly what it was, rolling hills of raised bog and bulrushes. What makes it really interesting, though, is that Sliabh Luachra is technically not 'on the map': it exists only in the mind of the people who live there. To them, Sliabh Luachra flows loosely over the hills and across the borders of the three counties that meet there, Cork, Kerry and Limerick. I remember, at an outside radio broadcast in Killarney back in 2001, the legendary box-player Johnny Leary of Gneeveguilla told me that Sliabh Luachra was 'more a state of mind than a place, actually'. Beautifully put.

THE OLD MEASURES

Gneeveguilla in Irish is Gníomh go Leith. A *gníomh* was an old form of land measurement. It was one-twelfth of a ploughland – the area of grass for one cow. Gneeveguilla therefore means 'an area of grass for one and a half cows'.

The late legendary storyteller Tim 'the Tailor' Buckley, from Garrynapeaka, always maintained that the old measures were best, simply because they indicated the real value of the land. With a *gníomh* you knew what you had, because it was a very real measure. It's true for him too. After all, 'a thousand acres' is no real indication of its worth. You might as well be buying a bag of beans!

I should add here that Garrynapeaka, or Gaorthadh na Péice, as it's written in Irish, was translated as 'garden of the sprout'. While *garraí* means a garden or vegetable patch, I would contend that Garrynapeaka could also be interpreted as 'a peak in a wooded area of river'. I feel that would fit the bill, and is probably a more accurate description of the area. After all, the nearest village, a few kilometres upstream, is Baile an Ghaorthaidh, meaning 'townland of the wooded river'. However, when it comes to *logainmneacha*, I've learned that there are often as many interpretations as spellings.

Either way, the Tailor Buckley took great pleasure in giving his full address as, 'Garrynapeaka, in the district of Inchigeelagh, in the parish of Uibh Laoghaire, in the barony of West Muskerry, in the county of Cork, in the province of Munster'. That's a large envelope already covered, and he still hadn't got to the Ireland bit of the address!

On another occasion in Sliabh Luachra I marvelled at these age-old tunes, handed down from one generation to the next. I listened to a melodeon player, John (Jack) Daly, father of world-renowned concertina player Jackie Daly, as he finished a set with a flourish. My colleague Peter Browne struck up a chat with John.

'Who handed down that last tune to you?' Peter enquired.

'Well, I actually got that tune from my son Jackie. He picked it up on his travels. So, I s'pose you could say 'twas handed up to me!' he replied, with a twinkle in his eye.

Interestingly, the memorised spoken word hasn't been entirely lost. The Fleadh Cheoil and Feiseanna still have competition categories for those who wish to recite the spoken word as a 'recitation'. Indeed, the principle is not exclusive to this island. I recall with great fondness, while trekking in Asia, the loud and repetitive recitation of the Koran emanating from the glassless windows of an Islamic boys' school in Tamil Nadu. On another occasion, when travelling through Israel, I witnessed young Jewish boys swaying from side to side, keeping time, as they rhythmically recited their prayers, verse by verse, for their teachers in a dimly lit holy place just beside the Wailing Wall in Jerusalem. It was hypnotic, dreamlike and somewhat surreal to be in the presence of knowledge being passed by word of mouth, as it has for centuries.

Mind you, as children, we too were forced to memorise long texts, poems and prayers in school. I still remember asking, 'But why are we learning it off by heart, Father, when we all own a copy of the book?'

The response was always the same.

'If it was good enough for your ancestors, then, by God, it's good enough for ye!'

And that was that.

In many schools today, texts are accessed online, and the skill of memorising words is quickly disappearing. I'm sometimes dismayed that the traditional Irish sing-song has often been reduced to a few half-hearted choruses at the 'afters' of a wedding, because nobody knows all the words of a song any more. Never mind our ancestors, the generation just before us would be shocked at how much music we have left to electronic devices, and how much knowledge we have left to instruction booklets and videos. Perhaps the jump from druid, to *bard*, to book, to Google isn't such a giant leap for mankind after all.

THE BARD'S TALE

The name 'Ward', whether it be the surname or a part of a place name, has noble origins that only become evident when you break down its Irish name, Mac an Bhaird.

Mac – son

An Bard – the bard (a professional storyteller)

Ward therefore means 'son of the bard'.

Similarly, to have 'bard' in a place name would also allude to the presence of bards in the area at one point. County Monaghan's Aghnamard is one such name that jumps to mind. In Irish, it is Achadh na mBard.

Let's break it down:

Achadh – field

Na mBard – (of) the bards

Aghnamard, then, translates as 'the field of the bards'.

Straight away I can picture scenes of these great storytellers surrounded by an attentive audience, eager to get the news and be entertained, not unlike our own generation gathered around a television. However, a name like 'the field of the bards' more likely alludes to the presence of bards on the battlefield. Indeed, the bards were often found at battle scenes, singing war songs and making mental records of words spoken to them by the very men who had fought in the battle.

DINDSENCHAS, THE LORE OF PLACES

The study of *logainmneacha* ranked highly in ancient Ireland and was considered a subject in itself. *Dindsenchas* ('the lore of places') was passed on by word of mouth. It recounts the origins, traditions, beliefs and mythology of place, with many valuable facts woven into the fabric of these most incredible tales. As this practice evolved during the Middle Ages, the *Dindsenchas* finally appeared in book form, with texts written in Old Irish and Latin. It's wonderful that, despite centuries of conflict on this island, these texts have survived, and when you pass through the language barrier, you discover a gold mine of knowledge, littered with nuggets of information about Ireland's geography and place names. A visit to Arigna's coal mines at Derreenavoggy in County Roscommon had me looking across Lough Allen at Sliabh an Iarainn ('the mountain of iron'), in Barnameenagh, County Leitrim. As the name suggests, that beautiful mountain has given of its bounty since the Iron Age.

The *Dindsenchas* didn't just take story form. Much of it was recalled in verse too, but whether recited as prose or verse, this priceless knowledge has been documented in the *Annála na gCeithre*

Máistrí ('Annals of the Four Masters') and subsequent writings. It's a living reference for us and those who come after us.

A classic example would be Tara in County Meath. During the Middle Ages, the King of Tara was seen as the King of Ireland, even though there was no such title then in existence, such was Tara's significance as a seat of power at the time. What we know about the significance of Tara, where its name came from, and even where its influence originated, is all revealed within the *Dindsenchas*.

WHO WAS TARA?

For many years, there have been considerable debates around the origins of the famous Irish place name Tara. The *Dindsenchas* would suggest that the name was derived from that of Princess Tea (pronounced 'Tia'). Her name, compounded with the noun *mor* from the Latin word *murus*, meaning 'wall', led to the creation of the name Teamhair, which was given to the site where she is said to be buried.

Translated, Teamhair means 'the burial mound of Tea'. So, who was she? And why do we still honour the place of her burial all these centuries later? Well, Tea was the daughter of the mythological King Lugaid, but she was also known as the wife of the chieftain ruler of Spain, Érimón. Érimón belonged to a Celtic race called the Milesians, known for their invasion tendencies, which comes as no surprise when you realise the source of the name Milesian. Milesian, which translates as 'sons of Míl', is derived from the term Míl Espáine, meaning 'soldiers of Spain'.

It is said that when Érimón wed Tea, he agreed to her request that he acquire a site of her choosing, and that this site would be, in time, not only her final resting place, but the site upon which royalty would reside thereafter. Not exactly your traditional wedding gift! Sure enough, in time, that's exactly what the Hill of Tara came to be: Tea's place of burial and also the country's seat of power. So why then, with their roots in Spain, did the couple choose Ireland? If the *Dindsenchas* is anything to go by, bloodshed, power and revenge is precisely what brought Érimón et al. to our isle. When you think about it, it was all very *Game of Thrones*.

THE BROTHERS GRIM

Although Érimón is said to have ruled Spain with his older brother, Éber Donn, they were not Spaniards. Érimón was born in Egypt, but the Milesians travelled extensively, and he and his family subsequently ended up in Spain. It would have quite possibly remained their home too, if only their beloved uncle, Íth, had not been killed by three kings of Ireland's mythical Tuatha Dé Danann.

Legend states that when Íth climbed Breogán's tower in A Coruña, a city in the Galicia region of north-west Spain, he looked out at the sea. It being a particularly clear day, Íth noticed a land far off in the distance. Curious to know who inhabited the island in question, he set off with the purpose of exploring it. As he approached the coastline, however, he was slain by three kings of the Tuatha Dé Danann. When Érimón and the Milesians learned of Íth's death, their blood boiled with fury, and immediately they took to the sea to try to find this island where Íth had taken his last breath. They intended to invade the island as revenge, but before they could begin battle, they had to first find the island in question. This quest, we are told, proved something of a struggle. The *Dindsenchas* suggests the Tuatha Dé Danann used their powers to make Ireland disappear from the sight of the Milesians, and certainly this wasn't beyond the realms of their mythological capability. I imagine the misty Irish climate may have also helped!

Eventually, the warriors found themselves within reach of Irish soil, but before they could make land, tragedy struck a second time. Érimón, along with his brother, Éber Donn, were said to have angered the Irish goddess Ériu, and as a result of their actions, Éber Donn drowned in a shipwreck. This happened not too far from the coasts of Kerry and Cork, as the *Dindsenchas* tells of Éber Donn being buried by his brothers on an island off the Beara Peninsula that became known as Teach Duinn. Today it's known as Bull Rock.

Now we need to veer a little off topic for a moment, because Teach Duinn merits its own explanation. There's a little code-cracking to be done with this name. In short, it translates as 'home of Donn'. It became known as such after Éber Donn was buried there, but in this situation 'Donn' refers to the old Celtic word Donn Fírinne, meaning the dark one, the dark lord or, to give the official title, 'God of the Dead'. A Donn Fírinne was essentially a fairy king, and if eighth-century sources are correct, Teach Duinn was where the souls of the dead were believed to gather before departing for the afterlife beyond the horizon of the known world. According to old writings reprinted by Dúchas, there exists an old Irish belief that the souls of the dead, when making their way to the other side, pass westwards over the sea towards the setting sun.

I think it's very possible that the unusual-looking portal-like cave that runs through Bull Rock is why this particular island was always associated with the legend of Donn Fírinne. Donn Fírinne himself was said to have dwelled underneath Knockfierna/Cnoc Fírinne (Truthful Hill) in County Limerick. Apparently, the entry to Donn Fírinne's abode was through a hole on the hillside, known as Poll na Bruidne. As I was looking into the folklore of Donn Fírinne, I came across a website with a quote from 'M O'Conchobhair of Ráth Caola (Rathkeale/Kealy's Fort) in Limerick', who apparently said, 'Donn lived in Knockfierna; the entrance to his palace was at Poll na Bruidne near the top of it. If you threw a cotton ball into Poll na Bruidne it would be returned to you with blood on it!'

This quote is certainly in keeping with the commonly held belief that if someone tested Donn Fírinne, he favoured a warning as opposed to a punishment. Interestingly, despite his name having such sinister connotations, Donn Fírinne is actually not thought to have brought harm to anyone unless they were deserving of it. In fact, folklore portrays him as being quite a generous, courteous man, who richly rewarded those who helped him or did him a good turn in some way.

There has also long been a legend that Donn Fírinne controlled the weather in the area around Knockfierna. If there were clouds over the hill, it was said that Donn Fírinne was gathering them together to make it rain. If there was a thunderstorm, locals would say Donn Fírinne was out riding his horse through the sky.

TEACH DUINN – TRANSLATED DIRECTLY FROM THE *DINDSENCHAS*

Tech Duinn, whence the name? Not hard to say. When the sons of Mil came from the west to Erin, their druid said to them, 'If one of you climbs the mast', said he, 'and chants incantations against the Tuatha De, before they can do so, the battle will be broken against them, and their land will be ours; and he that casts the spell will die.'

They cast lots among themselves, and the lot falls on Donn to climb the mast. So was it done: Donn climbed the mast, and chanted incantations against the Tuatha De, and then came down. And he said: 'I swear by the gods', quoth he, 'that now ye will not be granted

right nor justice.' The Tuatha De also chanted
incantations against the sons of Mil in answer
from the land. Then after they had cursed Donn,
there came forth with an ague into the ship. Said
Amairgen:

'Donn will die', said he, 'and it were not lucky
for us to keep his body, lest we catch the disease.
For if Donn be brought ashore, the disease will
remain in Erin for ever.' Said Donn: 'Let my
body be carried to one of the islands', said he,
'and my people will lay a blessing on me forever.'
Then through the incantations of the druids a
storm came upon them, and the ship wherein
Donn was foundered. 'Let his body be carried
to yonder high rock', says Amairgen: 'his folk
shall come to this spot.' So hence it is called
Tech Duinn: and for this cause, according to the
heathen, the souls of sinners visit Tech Duinn
before they go to hell, and give their blessing,
ere they go, to the soul of Donn. But as for the
righteous soul of a penitent, it beholds the place
from afar and is not borne astray. Such, at least,
is the belief of the heathen. Hence Tech Duinn is
so called.

Source: The Metrical Dindshenchas, poem/story 113, www.celt.ucc.ie

THE ORAL TRADITION

When the Milesians eventually made it to Irish soil, they embarked on a relentless battle, one which the *Dindsenchas* refers to as the Battle of Tailtiu. It was a battle that would see the Milesians reigning victorious and the Tuatha Dé Danann pagan kings being driven from prominence. Érimón was now free to rule in their place. Given the pre-battle demise of his older brother Éber Donn ('Brown/Dark Éber'), Érimón chose to rule Ireland alongside his younger brother, Éber Finn ('Blond Éber'). This resulted in the brothers dividing the country in two, with Érimón choosing the north and Éber Finn, the south.

To get a flavour of what the Milesian temperament was like, just consider what happened next. Unhappy with his lot, Éber Finn aired his grievances with Érimón, leading to the two brothers going to battle over the matter. Éber Finn lost his life, leaving Érimón as the sole ruler of Ireland, thus making him the first High King of Ireland.

The story of the Milesians and the Tuatha Dé Danann may seem far-fetched. How much of it is based on fact is anyone's guess, but I feel that within mythology, folklore and fairy tales there is often more than a kernel of truth. For example, Little Red Riding Hood has a valuable cautionary tale running through it. Little Red Riding Hood represents the child, the wolf represents the dangerous stranger, while the wood cutter represents the safe, responsible adult. When you impart the moral lesson through a narrative rather than instruction, you get a more attentive ear. Similarly, the 'Ring a Ring o' Rosie' nursery rhyme, which some say dates from the Great Plague, serves as a repeated mantra of health etiquette in a pandemic. It's hard to know if we will ever be able to confirm with absolute certainty if the origins of 'Ring a Ring o' Rosie' are in the bubonic plague, but the message is universal and timeless.

Ring-a-ring o' roses, (The roses represent the red, rash-like blotches on the skin.)

A pocket full of posies, (People would carry a posy of flowers or herbs in the belief that it would help protect them and others from the plague, as well as help ward off the pungent smell of the disease.)

A-tishoo! A-tishoo! (There are many variations of this nursery rhyme, and in some, the sentence reads as 'ashes, ashes'. Both are said to reference the plague symptom of fits of sneezing.)

We all fall down. (This is a reference to the mass deaths caused by the plague.)

In terms of the oral tradition, repetition in verse form was the best way of packaging information for people who could neither read nor write. Similarly, the storytelling of the *scéalaí* ('storyteller') and *seanchaí* ('reciter of ancient lore') were the night classes of earlier generations. A lecture is one thing, but if you begin your talk with 'Once upon a time ...' you have a captive audience!

COULD ATLANTIS BE IN IRELAND?

In 2004, Swedish academic Dr Ulf Erlingsson earned widespread derision when he claimed that Plato's description of the underwater kingdom of Atlantis matched Ireland, and that Tara in County Meath was its ancient capital. He later played down the theory, but it's an interesting notion. Imagine if, after all these years we've been believing Atlantis was somewhere under the sea, we were to discover that it was right in the middle of dear old Ireland.

ONCE UPON A TIME: STORIES FROM TARA

THE BLACK DOG AND THE PRIEST'S TREE

A black dog was said to guard the Hill of Tara. The dog was described as being larger than normal, and those who chanced upon the animal late at night recalled how it would actually walk along beside them. This all seemed quite harmless until I came across another story about the same dog. The Dúchas website has a remarkable story from an unnamed woman who recalls how her aunt and uncle were walking home one night when her aunt spotted the infamous dog just as they were passing the Priest's Tree on the Curtistown Road. (It appears that a priest by the name of Father O'Reilly was tragically killed there over 150 years ago, and since then it became known as 'The Priest's Tree'.) Anyway, according to the woman's account, her aunt cried out, 'Oh Ned, look at the black dog with fire out of his mouth!' Her husband, however, couldn't see the dog she was pointing at. The story concludes with the woman taking ill and passing away.

I remember hearing similar stories around West Cork when I was a boy. To this day, an animal is often portrayed as the harbinger of death. I've heard superstitions, from people much younger than me, about the significance of a robin entering a house or a butterfly making an appearance at a funeral. Then there's the one about good luck when a black cat crosses your path. I would imagine that a lot of lottery tickets were sold on the strength of Puss heading out on a date.

I expect it was born out of our need to make sense of the things we don't fully understand. When hard evidence is thin on the ground we are drawn to conjecture. When we lose a loved one, it's understandable that we might search for clues and clutch at straws.

A STONE IN FARRELL'S FIELD

I came across a wonderful account on the Dúchas website. Recorded back in 1938, it's typical of the wonderful *béaloideas* that was passed down through generations. Titled on the website as 'A Stone in Farrell's Field', the explanation of how it came to be there was given by a Meath man called Michael Byrd. Michael told of how this large stone featured what appeared to be a thumbprint, and interestingly he recalled two locally held beliefs of how the stone had found its way into this particular field. The first was that St Patrick had thrown the stone from the Hill of Tara, which was about five miles away, and that the thumbprint belonged to the saint himself. The second belief was that a mythological giant had thrown it from Tara. It's a short story, but it's enough to have you intrigued about how that stone really did end up there and who that thumbprint really does belong to.

TREASURE BENEATH YOUR FEET

In light of my earlier ponderings over the potential finds that lie in the muddy layers of the River Lee beneath St Patrick's Bridge, how could I not give some thought to the possible cache of treasures that exist beneath the soil of Tara? According to legend, treasure is exactly what is buried there. Burying gold and silver objects was the strongest way to safeguard valued articles from rogues and barbarians out for the take, particularly during times of war.

Of course, not all treasures there are buried. The famous standing stone, the Lia Fáil (Stone of Destiny), was said to have been one of the treasures brought to Tara by the Tuatha Dé Danann. The stone is believed to have been used as part of the coronation of Irish kings, with Celtic writings maintaining that should a true king stand on the stone it will let out an enormous roar. Given the significance of the stone itself, it makes you wonder what might potentially be buried underneath it!

HISTORY IN A NAME: TALLAGHT

By the sixth century, Irish monks were transcribing sacred texts, but interestingly they were also gathering secular material and committing it to vellum for posterity. We now have place names being recorded on paper at long last. It's from these annals that we find the earliest written records of *logainmneacha na hÉireann*.

One of the great revelations for me was discovering the meaning of Tallaght. The story behind the name makes fascinating reading, and must have made fascinating listening for those who still depended on the spoken word of the bards for their info!

The writer of *Lebor Gabála Érenn* (*The Book of Invasions*) gives an account of six invasions of Ireland from the time of the creation. It records that in the years following Noah and the deluge, Ireland experienced its third invasion. According to the book, an expedition from modern-day Sicily, in search of *terra firma*, landed in Ireland. This expedition was led by the Greek Partholón, and included his wife, three sons and 1,000 followers. They settled successfully in the Liffey Valley area, but 300 years later, 9,000 of Partholón's descendants died of plague within one week. Their name lives on, however, in the family name McPartlin, or Mac Parthalain in Irish, meaning descendants of Partholón. There are a number of variations on the family name, including McFarlane in Scotland. The plague grave that gives its name to modern-day Tallaght is the final resting place of the 9,000 plague victims. In fact, in 1836, Victorian scholars noted the place name was given locally as Taimhleacht Muintire Parthaloin. That's got to be 'the plague grave of the people of Partholón'.

- -
TALLAGHT, COUNTY DUBLIN
Tallaght – Tamhlacht
Támh (Tamh) – plague
Leacht – tombstone
We can take it that Tallaght therefore means 'the plague tombstone'.

Interestingly, the same *Book of Invasions* also tells us about the aforementioned Milesians, whom it records as having been responsible for Ireland's sixth, and final, invasion. Despite all the book-writing that was going on in the monasteries of Ireland, the bards successfully made the transition from their role in pagan, druidic society to the new Christian era, continuing to weave tales and disseminate wisdom for attentive ears. They plied their trade happily until the demise of Gaelic Ireland, which began with the defeat at the Battle of Kinsale in 1601. With the Flight of the Earls, the bards lost their patrons. In the following years, their position and influence waned to the point where their successors were seen as little more than travelling entertainers and labourers.

THE LAST OF THE BARDS

Dáibhí Ó Bruadair documented the demise of the great bardic tradition in his heartbreaking ode *D'Aithle Na bhFileadh* ('The High Poets are Gone'). The legendary blind harper Turlough O'Carolan, who died in Leitrim in 1738, is considered 'the last of the bards'.

BÉALOIDEAS

The tradition of passing knowledge by word of mouth did not disappear with the bards. Storytelling continued around the fireplaces of Ireland. Indeed, the modern Irish-language term for folklore is *béaloideas*. It's formed from two words: *béal* meaning 'mouth' and *oideas* meaning 'instruction'. In fact, if you look more carefully at these two words you get a better feel for the essence of the term *béaloideas*. To this day *oideas* is the commonly used Irish translation for 'a prescription' or 'a recipe', and I suppose *béaloideas* does offer the listener the recipes and remedies to life's challenges.

BÉALOIDEAS, A PRESCRIPTION FOR LIFE ITSELF

Old cures are a prime example of *béaloideas* at its finest. Way back before computers and Google, if you couldn't afford a doctor, the only way to find a cure for whatever ailed you was by word of mouth. The Dúchas website cites a 'Mrs Cochrane from County Cavan' who advised slicing a turnip, sprinkling some sugar on it and then drinking the juice as a cure for a cold. Another woman, a Mrs Blake from Tipperary, recommended eating treacle, while a lady from Tara Street in Dublin advised 'colds on lips rub with honey'. At least three times, I've encountered a cure that required the patient to eat boiled dandelion leaves. Rolling around in nettle leaves was also considered a treatment for rheumatism. While it's vital that we retain and pass on these folk remedies, it's also important to remember the old adage, 'Don't try this at home!' I won't. In fact, I'm off out this very moment to cut the nettles.

I'm reminded of our family trips to my mother's ancestral home in West Cork's Adrigole (Eadargóil, meaning 'between two inlets'). My Uncle Jack Michael and Aunty Kit lived with their two sons, Ronnie and Denis, on the coast road in Faha West (An Fhaiche Thiar, *faiche* meaning a grassy area or green).

These journeys almost always took place late in the day. The nature of my dad's work as a bus driver meant we couldn't leave any earlier, so sometimes it would be evening before we'd arrive at my cousins'.

Like most Irish families at the time, Jack and Kit didn't have a phone. However, the postcard my mother had sent some days earlier, saying 'Will be down to ye on Sunday, God willing', had both the household that sent it and the household that received it fussing in joyous anticipation. On the day, Jack Michael would be put on look-out duty. Resting his backside against the stone wall, he'd wait. Every now and then, Jack would light his Sweet Afton cigarette. Yes, one cigarette a day was the ration when times were tough. Jack Michael would allow himself a couple of draws at a time, and then would crush the glowing top between thumb and forefinger. This could happen five or six times over a day until he had the Sweet Afton sucked all the way to the fingernail. At the first sighting of my father's Zephyr coming over the horizon, Jack would be up off the wall, his cigarette topped in a shower of sparks, and with his collie Prince twirling in circles, he'd roar, 'They're here!'

I can still feel that flurry of excitement as we poured out of the car. The smiling faces of our beloved cousins Ronnie and Denis lit up as this exotic circus arrived from the city. Although we were all from the same county of Cork, they marvelled at our accents and we at theirs. Kit fousterin' in the kitchen, dusting around the fireplace with a goosewing, would greet us with, '*Dia linn*! Will you look at how you've grown! Come in! Come in! Ye're as welcome as the flowers in May!' Whenever Jack Michael stooped down to shake my little hand, I was always amazed by the size of his. It was strong but gentle; he was like John Wayne. God, we loved them, our cousins.

More than anything, I recall the smells from those times. As the car doors were thrown open, the perfume of wild woodbine in the ditch and the sweet scent of the hay from the shed flooded the warm summer air around us. We followed our noses through the evaporating paraffin in the back kitchen, through that beautiful, sour smell of burning turf in the fire, to the freshly baked brown cake on the table and salty rashers sizzling on the pan. We were wild on the freedom; climbing the hay reek, running back and forth to the henhouse to find eggs that weren't there the last time we checked – 'Look, Kit! I got one! I got one!' – before heading down to the hollow to stuff little fistfuls of hay under the soft muzzle of Uncle Jack's huge white mare, Pet. Any man who names his horse and working companion 'Pet' needs no further character reference from me. They were kind to each other.

Before it got dark, we'd gallop off down through the meadow like cowboys and Indians. In a field to the east of the house we'd kick the new ball we brought from the city. I still remember that field was named An Cnocán, meaning 'the hillock'. Needless to say, you were playing either uphill or downhill for each half of the game. One of my fondest memories is of Uncle Jack making sure to hold the cows back after milking so the city slickers could be farmers like their people before them. This was not your modern herd of Friesians. This was a multicoloured collection of exotica, each cow with its own name and backstory.

'Can we stampede 'em, Jack?' we'd plead.

'Ah 'twouldn't be right,' he'd say. 'Sure, they've been waiting half the day for ye to get here from Cork. Let them take their aize.'

And so, this little mixed herd of about a dozen cows of all breeds and none would sashay at their own pace through 'Fanrathán' and past 'The Garraí', a vegetable garden where potatoes and cabbages were once grown. Occasionally, the parade, which would be led by Strawberry, the prettiest dame in this bevy of beauties, would pause to nibble the sweetgrass on their way towards the sea field by 'Sawheelna'. My cousin Denis and I have promised to drill down into the spellings and original meanings of the field names at Faha. These minor names, as they're called, can play a major part in a person's life. They certainly featured large in the lifetime's work of Jack Michael.

Anyway, once the cattle were safely returned to the meadow beside Sawheelna, we'd take in the sea air and stare out at Siorrach, a sea stack just a few metres offshore at high tide. Hundreds of thousands of years of coastal erosion had whittled this headland back to just a narrow tower of land. It stood maybe 30 feet above the high-tide mark and was topped by a little green patch of grass.

'Could you put a cow or even a calf up there on Siorrach, Jack? Just to get the value out of the grass, like?'

'Yerra, 'twouldn't feed a goose, boyeen! But 'tis well known that one of the O'Sullivans danced a jig at the top of it when he won a medal for dancing at the Feis in 1911. He used to practise there on a good flat stone. You can still see where he chiselled his name, D. Ó Súilleabháin, into the rock. But sure, the sea will have the last word with Siorrach.'

Yes, like the people of Beara, Siorrach has proven its resilience and still stands defiantly against wind, rain and tide. Ultimately the rising seas and increasingly vicious storms will have their way, and Siorrach will eventually return to the seabed from which it first rose, just like Jack, Kit, my parents and all the old people have returned to the earth from which they came. God, I miss them.

> ### SEA HORSES AND FOALS
>
> The name Searrach or Siorrach is not unusual around the Irish coast. In West Kerry there are two close together, Siorrach and Máthair an tSiorraigh, which locals translate respectively as 'the foal' and 'the foal's mother'. There is also a series of sea stacks off the Mayo coast known locally Na Siorracha, meaning 'the small pinnacles'.

What I didn't realise as a child is that we were actually living the *béaloideas*. As the evening wore on and our eyes grew tired from staring at stars in the ink blackness of the Atlantic sky, we'd lift the latch and drift back indoors, where the heat from the turf fire would cradle you like a mother's embrace. Sleepy-eyed, we'd gather on the stairs that led straight up from the kitchen. This was a great perch to observe the court in session below. The conversation mostly centred around connections and 'placing people'.

'*Aon trácht* [any report] on the Sullivans?'

'Which Sullivans would that be?'

'The Castletowns.'

There were so many O'Sheas and O'Sullivans that most would be referred to by their townland. In this case, it was a family in Castletownbere that was related to my mother.

'Oh yes, Connie Batt is doing great now. Father John is home at the moment.'

'One of the boys ordained with him is gone out to Africa. Kenya, I think.'

'Which lad would that be?'

'The lad from Tyrone … Omagh, I think. He had a brother in the bank.'

'Were they McElvaneys or something?'

'No, no, McElhinney. The sister was a teacher.'

'That's right, I have you now. Wasn't their mother's people originally from over Ardgroom direction?'

'Aw-haw, that's right. Sullivans, too, but no connection to the Castletowns.'

From the comfort of Kit's fireplace in Adrigole we had travelled to Kenya, to Omagh and back home by way of Ardgroom in the hills just behind us, tracing the lives of people we had never met in places we were unlikely to ever visit. This is the *seanchas*.

From ancient times, the practice of memorising family connections and allies had a practical function in terms of keeping marriage records and, of course, the security of strength in numbers. These long, winding conversations were reassuring.

'Are ye all being good boys and girls up there?' my mother would enquire, prompted by the silence from on high.

No reply.

'Yerra, they've drifted off, the craturs,' my mother would say. 'I'll go up and throw a blanket over them. They'll have a right *tromchodladh* [heavy sleep] on them from all the running around. They'll sleep solid in the car going home.'

As I drifted in and out of consciousness, the muffled mantra of place names and people-placing drifted through the tongue-and-groove ceiling and floorboards beneath my ear.

I'd usually come round, several hours later, in the back seat of the Zephyr with a dead leg as I tried to untangle myself from the heap of sleeping children.

'Are we nearly home?' I'd croak.

'No, *petín bán*,' would come my mother's reply. 'We're only passing Johnny the Cross now. Go back to sleep.'

Like his namesake, this 'John of the Cross' was also a saintly man. He was elderly, quite frail and lived alone over his little shop, the kind where you could buy a bar of Cadbury's chocolate or a calf bucket. His 'shopeen' was only a mile or so from Faha West, at the first crossroads on the way home. I'd drift in and out of sleep, desperately trying to stay awake to hear the comforting hum of my parents' conversation as they pieced together the jigsaw of our people. My mother ached for Crooha, her childhood home and ancestral cradle in the hills above the coast road. Her younger sister Christina, who we called Aunty Dinah, was the last of the ten Blake sisters still living there.

'The light is still on in Trafrask. I suppose the Careys might have a cow calving.'

'I s'pose there's no point calling to Crooha at this hour, Connie? Gerry and Dinah might still be up.'

'They might, but we'd wake the children, Siobhán, and our own scholars have to be up in the morning too.'

'Well, we'll call first thing the next time so, Connie.'

'We will, and you'll have us out half the night again. God, I don't know how I tempted you down off that mountain at all. It must have been my good looks and swanky car, hah?'

'Hmm. Be more in your line to slow down. I'm serious, Connie, there was always a *piseog* [curse] on this stretch of road.'

'Sure, I know well, didn't Timmy Pheig tell me some poor boy in a truck went in over the ditch there only last year.'

'Isn't that a fright to God? Well, the divil fire it anyway, whatever old *mí-ádh* [misfortune] is on the place.'

TRAFRASK, WEST CORK
Trafrask – Trá Phraisce
Trá – strand/beach
Praiseach – sea kale
Trafrask therefore means 'the beach of the sea kale'.

On and on the conversation would flow, in the glow of the dashboard, as we made our journey home, taking in places like Snave/Snámh, where the cattle had to swim across the river before the bridge went in. Ballylickey would be next, and at some point I'd hear a verse of 'Bantry Bay' being sung quietly by my mother. As the miles wore on, there'd be a story about the day we got drenched fishing at a spot on the river known as Tadhg Manning's Hole. Coosán would be the next signpost on the journey, and there'd be talk of old friends like Jack Seán Rua. On past Graigue … Johnny Timmy Johnny's shop in darkness … a verse or two of the 'Inchigeelagh Lass' calling me to sleep. Then, without warning, the sharp city streetlights would pierce the dream, and the magic escaped. And then school in the morning.

I miss my parents' voices and the sound of once-familiar names, but I find consolation in the most unlikely places. The rhythm of the shipping forecast on my bedside radio is now my late-night journey home. The softly spoken 'Malin, Rockall, Rossan Point, Erris Head, Loop Head, Valentia, Mizen' now calls me to sleep.

I've also come to love a rosary recited at pace. It leaves no time or space for thoughts to get in, just the steady beat of an oral tradition that brings me back to equilibrium. Similarly, I returned to Beara recently for a clifftop Buddhist retreat at Dzogchen Beara. At day's end, I sat on a whitewashed wall outside the meditation hall looking at the little Buddhist prayer flags fluttering in a mild south-westerly breeze. The melting sun slowly dripped beneath the Atlantic and I could hear the low, gravelly sound of Tibetan monks rhythmically chanting. I was carried with it to the *Dindsenchas* of my own ancestors and the *béaloideas* of my childhood.

In the beginning was the word ... and it was spoken.

3

WHAT DID THE GREEKS AND ROMANS EVER DO FOR US?

Ireland is a relatively new name for this place we call home. I expect the earliest settlers here didn't view it as a 'country' as such. Clearly, it wasn't a political or a civil unit, but rather a series of clan territories. The island of Ireland went through a variety of name changes before it appeared as 'Ireland'. Back in 320 BC, its name was given as 'Ierne', and the first person to document its presence on the periphery of Europe was a Greek geographer and explorer called Pytheas, or Pytheas of Massalia, to give him his full title, or even his full place name!

PYTHEAS

Pytheas, to his credit, embarked on what was a remarkably brave voyage. Travelling north from the Mediterranean, he sailed with a view to exploring the strange lands which, in the minds of his contemporaries, only existed in Greek myth and legend. As a merchant, Pytheas was also on the lookout for precious metals to trade. Tin, being one of the rarest and therefore of considerable value, was likely the real catalyst for his quest. Unfortunately, not much is known about what Pytheas saw.

He reportedly wrote a book about his voyage, but it has never been found, so when Pytheas died, everything he witnessed during his travels died with him. The only information we have is based on the writings of other ancient explorers who knew Pytheas, or were familiar with his written work. There are accounts, however, that can be safely considered reliable. It is generally accepted, for instance, that Pytheas sailed from Massalia, through the Pillars of Hercules (which today we know as the Strait of Gibraltar), before then heading north, past the beautiful coastlines of Spain and Portugal. It is likely he docked along the way, but this will only ever be speculation. Pytheas is believed to have then sailed towards Britain, landing in what we know today as Cornwall. Clearly, he remained here for some time, as ancient scripts tell of the observations he made regarding the locals, their living conditions and the culture in general.

Debate still swirls around whether or not he actually set foot on Irish soil. Personally, I'd like to think he did. What reason would he have had for not doing so? What we do know for sure, however, is that he referred to Ireland as 'Ierne', meaning 'abundant one'. I often wondered if that was where the Dublin-based Ierne Ballroom of my youth got its name!

It is believed that Pytheas subsequently sailed northwards to Iceland and even further on into the Arctic Ocean. He reportedly witnessed the mighty ice sheet, a staggering revelation for an ancient Greek. Today he is widely regarded as having been the first Mediterranean explorer to reach the Arctic. Can you imagine how terrifying, and how alien, that landscape must have seemed to a Greek explorer back in 320 BC? At least the Apollo astronauts knew what the moon's surface would look like when they got there! Incidentally, there are some Irish place names in outer space, but more of that later …

To this day, reported findings from his voyage are fraught with doubt, and will continue to be the subject of heated debates amongst scholars. Pytheas had his critics in his own lifetime too, and they certainly didn't spare him. One Greek astronomer, Strabo, was even said to have called him 'the very worst of liars', though I have a feeling that Strabo's remarks might well have been motivated by a little begrudgery. Given what we now know about the Arctic and the shape of the planet, it's likely Strabo was a paid-up member of the Flat Earth Society. Either way, few can dispute that Pytheas's voyage was a considerable adventure. My award for explorer of the year 320 BC goes to Pytheas, who risked falling off the edge of the planet as he sailed to Ierne and beyond!

CLAUDIUS PTOLEMY

A few centuries after Pytheas, this island came under the scrutiny of another Greek. In AD 140, roughly a hundred years after the crucifixion of Jesus, the mathematician, astronomer and cartographer Claudius Ptolemy is said to have created the very first map of our country. The map was based on Roman military charts and measurements taken from sea. Good man, Claude! I mean, up to that point, there did not exist an actual map of Ireland. A difficult scenario to envisage. Imagine living in Ireland back in AD 140 and not knowing its actual shape, size or what was going on up the other end? There's an element of doubt over whether Ptolemy actually spent any time in Ireland, but if he did, and if he walked the boggy landscape, it must have been some eye-opener for him, especially when you consider he had spent most of his life in the searing heat of Egypt. I expect it was a shock to the senses, surpassed only by Pytheas stumbling upon the Arctic. Is it any wonder the Romans named this island Hibernia, meaning the land of winter!

IOUERNIA VS IERNE

Ptolemy referred to this island as 'Iouernia', not a million miles removed from 'Ierne', the name recorded by Pytheas half a century earlier. Sometime later, in his book *Agricola*, the Roman scholar Tacitus referred to the country as 'Hibernia'. So you can see the name for Ireland slowly evolving, and this is exactly what happens to both major and minor place names. They get misspelled, they get translated, they get lost in translation, and slowly, over time, they change form. It goes back to what I was saying earlier: words are organic and can take many shapes. The roots tend to remain the same, however.

PTOLEMY'S MAP TRANSLATED

Can you just imagine the voice inside your GPS trying to pronounce some of these ancient names? While no one can say with absolute certainty that the following list is a definitive interpretation of the places and peoples identified by Ptolemy, it is interesting to see if you can make any connections.

- ▷ Argita – Lough Swilly
- ▷ Ausoba – Galway Bay
- ▷ Birgus – River Barrow
- ▷ Boreum – Bloody Foreland, County Donegal
- ▷ Bouvinda – River Boyne
- ▷ Dabrona – River Lee, Cork
- ▷ Dunum – Downpatrick, County Down
- ▷ Duris – Tralee Bay
- ▷ Eblana – Dublin

- ▷ Hibernis – Kenmare, County Kerry
- ▷ Isamnium – County Down
- ▷ Laberus – Rathconrath, County Meath
- ▷ Libnius – Garavogue River
- ▷ Logia – River Foyle or River Lagan
- ▷ Magnata – Sligo
- ▷ Menapia – Wexford Town
- ▷ Modonnus – River Slaney
- ▷ Raiba/Riba – Uisnech, County Meath
- ▷ Ravius – River Erne
- ▷ Regia – likely St Patrick's Purgatory, Lough Derg
- ▷ Regia – Longford
- ▷ Rhaeba Rheban – Athy
- ▷ Rhobogdium – Malin Head
- ▷ Sacrum – Hook Head
- ▷ Senus – River Shannon
- ▷ Vennicnium – Horn Head (but could possibly mean Fanad Head)
- ▷ Vinderis – Antrim

- - - - - - - - - - - - - - - - - -

KENMARE, CO KERRY
Kenmare – Ceann Mara/Neidín
Ceann – Head
Muir (Mara) – Sea
Ceann Mara means 'head of the sea' (i.e. of the flood tide).
Neidín means 'little nest'.

OBOKA, COUNTY WICKLOW

Did you know that a well-known village in County Wicklow is said to have got its name from Ptolemy's map? Ptolemy referred to the River Oboka on his map, which many now believe to be the River Liffey. However, a misinterpretation of the name Oboka many generations later is said to have resulted in Avoca being so named. Its Irish name is Abhóca. The river flowing through the village was formerly Abhainn Mhór, meaning 'big river'. Interestingly, Avoca is one of the most commonly occurring Irish names on the maps of other countries. Have a read of 'How did our names get on their maps?' later in this book.

THE CELTS AND THE BIRTH OF NATURE'S SIGNPOSTS

Farmers get a bad rap. In most modern cultures, it seems the farmer is often relegated to the role of unsophisticated peasant and the butt of many jokes. Here's the thing, though. The Celts were farmers, but they were no fools. They had a sophisticated social and civil society. Although they were migratory tribes to begin with, in Ireland they settled into a tightly knit jigsaw of clan territories, each with its own king. As society settled and evolved, the long, wet winter nights spent by the fire, sheltering from the elements, must have provided the cocoon in which our language and rich oral tradition developed.

Once settled, the naming and memorising of their places and territories began. For thousands of years, Ireland's place names were mostly concerned with simple topographical features.

Natural landmarks include:

- ▷ Cnoc (Knock) meaning hill
- ▷ Loch (Lough) meaning lake
- ▷ Carraig (Carrig) meaning rock
- ▷ Beann (Ben) meaning peak
- ▷ Cluain (Clon) meaning meadow
- ▷ Doire (Derry) meaning oak grove
- ▷ Gleann (Glen) meaning valley

Even a simple word like *cloch*, which means 'stone', lends itself to Na Clocha Liatha, meaning Greystones, now a busy commuter town on the coast of County Wicklow.

Burial mounds and pagan religious sites began to appear on the Irish landscape and were incorporated into this 'map of the mind'. I like to think that the very first 'signposts', if you will, were ogham stones. These first appeared in the fourth century, and were written in a script that pre-dates Old Irish by about three centuries. For the most part, they were marker stones, bearing the name of the deceased and detailing from whom they were descended, using early forms of the term *mac*, meaning son. We now had a written record of whose territory we were standing in, and while not 'signposts' per se, they appear at a significant crossroads in the evolution of Irish place names. The imprint of human hand will increasingly feature on the names of our places.

Ireland has numerous ogham stones, particularly in the south-west. Others have been found in parts of Wales, which was once colonised by settlers from Ireland. The Isle of Man is also home to quite a few ogham stones, as is Scotland, although many of the Scottish stones feature the language of the native Picts. Interestingly, a few of the English stones display some Christian and Roman references, so their creation came a little later, probably chiselled from the fifth century onwards, I would say. Remember, Britain, unlike Ireland, was governed by the Roman Empire. So in AD 313, Emperor Constantine decided to allow Christian practice, and subsequently converted to Christianity himself. When the emperor became Christian, the path was cleared for others to follow. That's the way it is with empires.

Ireland became Christian and embraced the Gospels, independent of Rome. Indeed these 'insular Christians' of Ireland and western Scotland remained unaligned to Rome for many centuries to come – the Independent People's Popular Front of Christianity, as it were (with apologies to Monty Python).

Sometimes it's difficult to separate natural features from man-made. Take Ardrahan in County Galway. It is exactly what it says on the signpost, depending on how you read it:

It's either, 'hill of the ferns' or 'little ring-fort on a height'.

Let's break it down:

Ardrahan is given in Irish as Ard Raithin.

'Ard' means 'raised' or 'height, hillock'

'Raithin' means 'ferns' (from *raithní*)

However:

'Rath' (or *ráth*) means 'fort'

'ín' denotes the diminutive

A thousand years after it was named, you can still see the remnants of an old structure, and a few ferns, up on a hump, on your right-hand side, as you drive northwards to Galway. As there is no *síneadh fada* over the letter 'I' in the Irish form of the name, I'm inclined to favour 'ferns' over 'little fort'.

Increasingly, human construction was incorporated into *logainmneacha*. For example, *caisleán*, meaning 'castle', became commonplace. So too were words such as *droichead*, meaning 'bridge', and *tóchar*, meaning 'a causeway or a raised road'. The word *tóchar* springs up in a variety of place names around the country, both as a name in itself and as part of a name. A fine example would be Limerick's Kantoher. If you were to break it down, you would first translate Kantoher into Irish, which would give you Ceann Tóchair. With *ceann* meaning 'head' and *tóchar* meaning 'causeway', Kantoher therefore means 'the head of the causeway'. All a matter of cracking that code.

ROCK OF THE MEN

I attended secondary school at Coláiste an Chroí Naofa, Carraig na bhFear, which literally translates as 'Rock of the Men'. The school was situated on lands once owned by the McCarthy clan, and even boasted the substantial remnants of an old McCarthy castle. A double maths class on a lazy afternoon would see me drift off, dreaming of romantic dalliances prompted by Shakespeare's *Romeo and Juliet* from that morning's English class. Soon after, I would be suddenly roused from my reverie by a belt of the teacher's duster and his battle cry, 'Wake up! Carraig na bhFear … The Rock of the Men … some bloody men ye are!'

By the early Gaelic period, we have mythology, landscape, physical structures, family names, plants and animals colouring the place names of Ireland. Yes, as you might expect, domestic animals played a huge part in our culture. We were farmers, remember?

Examples are scattered across the map of Ireland, like:

▷ Drumshanbo – Droim Seanbhó (Leitrim) – the ridge of the old cow, or cow sheds.

▷ Poulacapple – Poll an Chapaill (Tipperary/Clare/Galway) – no, not 'the horse's hole', as Ray D'Arcy once suggested to me, but rather the hollow where the horse was kept!

I love to stop and consider the actual animal that was the subject of a place name. I mean, I still feel for that poor oul' horse of Poulacapple, as he returned to his own little glen following his last day's toil. It's beautiful that he is remembered forever by having a place name dedicated to him, despite the sneers of an oul' blow-in like D'Arcy with his fancy Norman name. Ha! I'm with the horse on this one!

Not only were the Celts farming people, who guarded and revered their livestock, they were also remarkable storytellers. Television had yet to be invented, so in the hours of darkness, stirring tales of prize bulls, serpents, legendary cattle raids like the *Táin Bó Cúailnge* (*The Cattle Raid of Cooley*), along with wise old tales like the one about the Salmon of Knowledge (*An Bradán Feasa*), were recounted amidst the glowing sparks of the bonfire.

To this day, the *seanchaí* – from *sean* ('old') and *caoi* ('way') – give accounts of major events from the locality, folk tales and fairy tales. By comparison, the *scéalaí*, literally 'the storyteller', was held in the highest regard, and was the repository of long epic tales and sagas. I often wonder how many of the Viking sagas were traded for our epic Irish tales as the Norsemen settled amongst people with a similar love of long stories for long nights.

HONOURED IN PLACE AND NAME

Wild animals that have disappeared from the Irish countryside now survive only in our place names. These *logainmneacha* serve as a record that these beasts did once roam our forests. There are many fine examples, such as:

▷ The Eagle's Nest – Nead an Iolair, County Cork

▷ The Place of the Boars – Log na gCollach/Lugnagullagh, County Westmeath

▷ Eagle Island – Oileán an Iolair, County Sligo

▷ The Boar's Head – Ceann Toirc/Kanturk, County Cork.

Interestingly, the boar's head in this place name refers to the coat of arms of the local McDonagh branch of the McCarthy clan.

I love the Irish-language term for 'wolf'. It's *mac tíre*, which translates as 'son of the countryside'. This name suggests a healthy respect, if not an affection, for this powerful beast.

The modern-day Irish word for dog, *madra*, was also once used in the broader sense to include the wolf. References to wolves appear in this form in numerous Irish place names. Take, for example, Limavady (Léim an Mhadaidh), meaning 'the leap of the dog/wolf', and of course Poulawaddra (Poll an Mhadra), meaning 'hole or hollow of the dog/wolf'. But please don't tell D'Arcy about that one!

Indeed, the fox is widely known as both *an madra rua* (meaning 'the red dog') and sometimes as *sionnach*. This wily creature also features on numerous Irish maps. A friend of mine lives in the townland of Carrigeenshinnagh in County Wicklow. In Irish, this translates as Carraigín na Sionnach, which means 'the little rock of the foxes'. However, she prefers the more upwardly mobile mistranslation of 'Little Foxrock'. Now, as rocks go, that's posh!

Here are a few more place names where the wolf makes an appearance:

▷ Wolfhill – Cnocán na Mac Tíre, County Laois

▷ Toom – Tuaim na Mac Tíre, County Wexford, meaning 'the burial place of the wolves'

▷ Isknamacteera – Eisc na Mac Tíre, a lake in County Kerry, meaning 'water of the wolves'

▷ Knockaunvickteera – Cnocán an Mhic Tíre, County Clare, meaning 'little hill of the wolf'

While animals like the Irish wolf may have been hunted to extinction, thankfully, their memory is preserved forever in our place names – that is, as long as the place names themselves don't become extinct. This is another reminder of how valuable our place names are. You see, *logainmneacha* are repositories not only for our history, but for our natural history too.

BULLS AND SWANS

Another animal that frequently pops up in Irish place names is the bull (*tarbh*). We have the obvious places like Dublin's Bull Island and the nearby Clontarf, the Irish translation of which is Cluain Tarbh, meaning 'the meadow of the bulls'.

Swans, likewise, decorate the place names of Ireland. Near my father's home place in West Cork, there is a stretch of water called Annahalla, or River Allow, which is given in Irish as Abhainn Ealla, meaning 'the river of the swans'. There could be as many as 80–100 swans gathered there any time we drove by on our way to visit family in Inchigeelagh. We would be on the lookout for them, and when they emerged from beyond the bridge the revelation was dramatic. To witness a flotilla of swans gliding by so gracefully can be truly awe-inspiring. To this very day you will find swans there, and I still marvel at the idea that the ancestors of these swans we see on Abhainn Ealla today were paddling through that same water centuries ago. Clearly, they were there in large-enough numbers to have inspired the 'place namers' to call it thus. As a small boy I used refer to the area as 'the swanny river', not realising that a thousand years earlier, other little boys were probably calling it the same thing. As an adult, I now wonder if any of those children were my own ancestors. I'm still prone to the odd lump-in-the-throat moment when I find myself thinking about things like that, and the people who have gone before us.

Ireland's place names suggest that our ancestors had a great love and understanding of nature. From the moment my father explained to me the meaning of Tír na Spideoige ('land of the robin'), it was clear to me that my people had a real *grá* for every living thing that shared this place with them, right down to the smallest of birds in the hedgerows. If further evidence was ever needed, just look at how common the minor place name 'Cúinne an Ghiorria' is on Irish farms. Cúinne an Ghiorria, which means 'the hare's corner' (or 'the corner of the hare') is the name given to the corner of a field. Traditionally, when farmers were harvesting, they would avoid mowing into the very corner of the field, and instead make a wide turn so that some high grass remained. This was done with a view to leaving a safe place for the hare. On some farms today, you'll still find an area known as Cúinne an Ghiorria.

On a completely unrelated note, I always thought the name *giorria* was a beautiful name for an animal. *Giorr*, or *gearr*, means 'short', while *fia* means 'deer', so together *giorria* means a short deer, which, when you think about it, is the perfect description for a hare!

DROMTARRIFF, COUNTY CORK
Dromtarriff – Drom Tairbh
Drom – hump, or hill
Tarbh (Tairbh) – (of the) bull
Dromtarriff therefore means 'hill of the bull'.

PIGS IN PLACE NAMES

The Irish word *muc*, meaning 'pig', pops up regularly on signposts at crossroads all over the country. I once had a friend, now long gone, who lived on a narrow byroad in Muskerry. Her address was Bóthar Chac na Muc. No visitor in their right mind ever made any reference to its translation (Pig Shit Lane). Thank God for the new Eircode! Whenever I pass that way these days I smile to myself as I think of the reception place-name pioneer John O'Donovan might have received when he arrived at the cottage door enquiring about the place name and how it might be transliterated. I expect he was given his answer on the end of a sharp tongue and a sharper dung-fork!

ROSMUC, COUNTY GALWAY
Ros – Woodland
Muc – Pig
Rosmuc therefore means 'the woodland of the pigs'.

PLACE NAMES INSPIRED BY ANIMALS

▷ Lisnageeragh, Longford – Lios na gCaorach – 'fort of the sheep'

▷ Inchnamuck, Tipperary – Inse na Muc – 'river-meadow of the pigs'

▷ Tankardstown, Meath – Bóithrín na Muice – 'little road of the pig'

▷ Drumcappul, Waterford – Drom Capaill – 'horse ridge'

▷ Tobernagat, Clare – Tobar na gCat – 'the cat's well'

▷ Clonmel, Tipperary – Cluain Meala – 'the meadow of the honey'

▷ Catfort, Mayo – Cathair an Chait – 'fort of the cat'

▷ Carrignamaddry, Cork – Carraig na Madraí – 'rock of the dogs'

▷ Kylespiddoge, Laois – Coill na Spideog – 'the wood of the robins'

▷ Pig Island, Kerry – Oileán na Muice – 'the pig's island'

▷ Graiguenaspiddoge, Carlow – Gráig na Spideog – 'hamlet of the robins'

GAIRDÍN NA LASRACHA COILLE

One of my favourite Irish animal names is *lasair choille* ('goldfinch'). Unlike the wolf and the eagle, it has no place name to celebrate its beauty. What a shame. The goldfinch has a little scarlet-red face with a white ring around it, a copper-coloured back with cream underbelly and spotted navy/black and white tail feathers. Quite exotic, but there's even more. Under the wings are hidden the brightest canary-coloured feathers. The collective noun for a group of goldfinches is 'a charm'. Apt, given the joy their colour brings to the countryside. When you see a goldfinch in flight, the first thing you notice is that bright flash of yellow ... that little glint of gold as they open their wings and shoot past.

The direct translation of *lasair choille* is 'spark of light of the woods'. Thanks to the thistles and the occasional offering of nyjer seed from my bird feeder, a fine charm of goldfinches now visits my back garden. Although I have searched the map of Ireland, I have yet to find a place name that honours this native beauty. So I've decided to take matters into my own hands, and at the time of writing, the place formerly known as 'out the back' has been renamed 'Gairdín na Lasracha Coille'!

CAVE OF THE CATS

One of our most unusual *logainmneacha* has got to be Roscommon's Cave of the Cats (Oweynagat, from Uaimh na gCat) at the historical site of Rathcroghan. Irish mythology suggests Oweynagat was the birthplace of Queen Medb, but its fame, or infamy as the case may be, stems from its reputation as a portal to hell! Of all the strange things you might find in Roscommon, who would have thought the gateway to hell would be one of them! Rathcroghan, where Oweynagat is located, is actually credited as the site where Samhain originated, a festival which today is better known as Halloween.

The origins of Samhain, it is claimed, lie in Oweynagat, where mythical monsters and spirits of the deceased left the 'other world' to enter the land of the living. Legend also claims that the cave's power as a portal to hell was at its strongest around Samhain/Halloween, when the line between the two worlds was a very fine one.

I visited Oweynagat in 2019 for the television series *Creedon's Atlas*. Producer Barry Donnellan, assistant cameraman Colin Morrison and I spent several hours in the darkness of this underworld, and I can understand how the Celts could have viewed the main chamber as nature's womb. The light hurt my eyes as we finally emerged through a narrow fissure into the world above ground. As I pulled myself forward, on my belly, through rock that had been worn smooth by the hands of others before me, I felt a real connection with those curious enough to enter this 'other world' throughout the millennia.

Indeed, there's a wide variety of tales about Oweynagat, but one that really captured my interest was recorded from a Roscommon man named John Boland and documented on the Dúchas website. This, to me, is a fine example of *béaloideas* in action.

> *A few miles from my residence lie the historic*
> *plains of Rathcroghan which were formerly*
> *owned by Colonel Chichester. He also owned*
> *the estate on which my school is built. The*
> *meaning of the word Rathcroghan according*
> *to the ancients is O'Connor's Fort. Perhaps this*
> *name is derived from the time of the O'Connor*
> *kingship in this province. However, the place is*
> *noted for its caves which extend from there to*
> *the town of Boyle. Near the entrance to one is*

*the grave of King Daithi – the last pagan king of
Éire – who was buried in full regimentals with
his golden crown upon his head.*

*In the field where King Daithi was buried is a
very high fort and it has often been mentioned
in stories. The following is one of them. One
evening a man was out looking after his stock
when he saw a stranger near the fort. He moved
forward until he came in contact with the
stranger and then he inquired his business there.
The stranger said he came from the North of
Ireland, and that he heard from tradition that
there was a five ton gate covered with a foot
and a half of black clay the south side of the fort
and as much gold under it as it would take five
horses to draw. A serpent guarded this treasure.
He observed it would be well worth getting but
life was dearer than gold. That night the stranger
dug but on reaching the gate a terrific wind
arose which so frightened him that he left all
there and fled in terror. Next morning the clay
was back again in its place as if untouched by
the hand of man.*

Source: The Schools' Collection, Volume 0262, Page 048

(www.duchas.ie) © National Folklore Collection, UCD.

Despite the origins of the cave's reputation being grounded
in mythology and legend, the fables associated with the site were
compelling enough to be taken seriously by the Church, with
Christian texts from the 18th century apparently describing the
cave as 'the hell-mouth of Ireland'.

Given that the Irish word *cath* does in fact mean 'battle', there remains some dispute over whether the name of the cave is actually meant to be Cave of the Battle as opposed to Cave of the Cats. That detail aside, however, the cave has always been known as the Cave of the Cats, and will no doubt continue to be referred to as such for many years to come.

4

CHRISTIANITY, MONASTICISM AND IRELAND'S PLACE NAMES

The hailstones were hopping off my head and stinging my rosy cheeks, but the Irish tricolour at the vanguard of two hundred boys and men had my undivided attention. Earlier, I had examined the network of cold-induced blue rings on my chubby thighs and reminded myself that a pelting of hailstones was a small penance to suffer in comparison to poor St Patrick, who, as I understood it at the time, was hung, drawn and quartered by the Brits. At eight years of age, I wasn't yet strong enough to carry a Lee–Enfield 303 rifle like my brother Don, who was standing to attention within the ranks of the older FCA lads. So, while I was still too young to die for Ireland, as a sworn-in member of the Macaoimh, this cub scout was definitely tough enough to brave the hailstones as I prepared to march in my first ever St Patrick's Day parade.

'*Buíon, Buíon, AIRE!*' roared the NCO. '*Do réir an chlé ... go mear ... MÁIRSEÁIL!*'

And we were off!

SAINT PATRICK

St Patrick featured large in the place names around my neighbourhood. St Patrick's Street, St Patrick's Bridge, St Patrick's Hill, St Patrick's Place, St Patrick's Church, St Patrick's Quay, and even a St Patrick's Credit Union, all to be found within a minute or two of our house. As I later discovered to my horror, however, Patrick wasn't killed by the Brits at all. He was actually one of them! A native of modern-day Wales, Patrick's own writings, gathered under the title *The Confessions of Patrick*, opens with the lines, 'I Patrick a sinner.' His writings reveal a humble man with deep affection for Ireland and the Irish. This is despite the fact that he had been captured by pirates when he was aged around 16 and sold into slavery to work as a shepherd for a farmer called Milchu. Patrick's shepherding duties took place on Antrim's Slemish Mountain/ Sliabh Mis, meaning 'the mountain of Mis'.

There is little doubt that Patrick was preceded by earlier Christian missionaries like Palladius, who arrived here from Gaul in 431. It's said that Patrick, after he escaped to Britain and was ordained, returned to Ireland in 432, although many scholars claim that this date was selected merely to acknowledge that Palladius 'got here first', so to speak, and to minimise the credit due to him and maximise the impact of our own national saint. Either way, the country was Christianised within the century by Patrick and the 12 apostles of Ireland who came after him and the female saints such as:

  ▷ St Brigit of Kildare/Cill Dara

  ▷ St Gobnait in Ballyvourney/Baile Bhuirne, County Cork

  ▷ St Ita of Limerick's Killeedy/Cill Íde, meaning 'Ita's church'

  ▷ St Attracta of Sligo's Lough Gara/Loch Uí Ghadhra and Tourlestrane/Tuar Loistreáin

  ▷ St Brónach of Kilbroney/Cill Bhrónaí, meaning 'Brónach's church', County Down

▷ St Trea of Ardtrea, meaning 'Trea's height or hill', County Derry

These remarkable women had such a profound impact on Irish monastic life, and left legacies so strong, their memories remain forever enshrined in a variety of names, from parishes and villages, churches and holy wells, streets, GAA clubs and schools, throughout the country.

▷ Tobar Ghobnait – St Gobnait's Well, County Waterford

▷ Bóthar Athracht – St Attracta's Road, County Dublin

▷ Coill Ghobnait – St Gobnait's Wood, County Cork

▷ Páirc Athrachta – St Attracta's Park, County Roscommon

▷ Ardán Bhríde – St Bridget's Terrace, County Meath

PLACES ASSOCIATED WITH ST PATRICK

DOWNPATRICK, ANTRIM

Downpatrick was originally just known as 'Down', taking its name from the Irish word *dún*, meaning 'fort'. 'Patrick' was subsequently added to the place name, thereby changing the meaning to 'Patrick's Fort' as a way of marking the abbey founded there by St Patrick. Incidentally, the name 'Down' was later given to the county itself. Down Cathedral, which overlooks the town of Downpatrick, is now the accepted burial site of St Patrick, with his final resting place at the highest point of Cathedral Hill.

ST PATRICK'S WELL, CLONMEL, TIPPERARY

The sacred site of St Patrick's Well is where the saint is said to have baptised hundreds of converts to the Christian faith. Interestingly, there remains a locally held belief that the water in the well never freezes over during the winter months.

DOWNPATRICK HEAD, MAYO

The famous sea stack sitting off the coast of North Mayo has a remarkable association with St Patrick, insofar as he is said to have created it! According to mythology, St Patrick built a church in the area and was familiar with a local pagan chieftain called Crom Dubh. Patrick had heard of the man's inexplicable cruelty and was keen to convert him to Christianity. Crom Dubh, however, wasn't overly excited about the idea and refused to buckle. Such was his disdain for Patrick that he snapped! He decided to throw poor Patrick into a fire that had been raging furiously near his fortress for eternity. Sounds like hell to me. Anyway, before Crom Dubh could do the drastic deed, Patrick picked up a small rock, upon which he scratched a cross. It's not what I'd have done, but he's the saint. Patrick then hurled this rock into the flames and immediately the fire fell into the sea forming a blowhole that is still known today as Poll a' Sean Tine, which in English translates as 'the hole of the ancient fire'. Seeing this, Crom Dubh fled to his fortress, but Patrick pursued him, committed to ensuring this pagan flame would never again be lit in Ireland. Patrick slammed his staff into the soil, thus causing the ground on which the fortress stood to break away from the headland as an isolated sea stack, which today is known as Dún Briste, meaning 'broken fort'. Crom Dubh was simply left there to die alone.

FLAMES OF PASSION

Variations on the same theme are found in the *Dindsenchas* all over Ireland. The struggles between the rival belief systems are often characterised by fire. Druidic fires had been central to many rituals in the old pagan calendar, and fire was also a symbol of the growing flames of passion for the new faith.

While filming the television series *Creedon's Epic East*, producer Tom Johnson arranged for us to witness a 'fire showdown' by community groups in County Meath. One huge bonfire was set on the Hill of Slane, where Patrick is said to have lit a Paschal fire ahead of the pagan fire on the nearby Hill of Tara. This bold act of challenging the old authority of the king and his druids is said to have been seen from Tara, which is quite a few miles away by road. Many have disputed the legend, saying that a bonfire on Slane could not be seen from Tara; however, the 'fire showdown' was an opportunity for us to put the theory to the test for the very first time.

Once the first few *cipíní* ('sticks') took hold at the Slane bonfire, Tom and myself dashed in my old Volkswagen campervan from one hill to the other, to see if we could see any trace at all of the Slane bonfire. If we could, and it seemed unlikely we would, given the size of the fire and the distance we had to cover, it would have lent considerable credence to this fantastic tale. We had our online compass and binoculars, but no show. Then, as if out of nowhere, a flicker of flame caught my eye. It was further along the ridge than the spot identified by the technology. Sure enough, in the dark of night we could see yonder Christian bonfire from druid HQ. No binoculars required.

The significance of fire loomed large in my Catholic childhood. There were the fires of hell and eternal damnation, where the likes of Crom Dubh are probably still adding fuel to the flames of shame burning in the cheeks of bold boys who couldn't remember their six times tables. Christian passion was also represented by fire, like the flame in the Sacred Heart of Jesus, who looked down compassionately from the wall of every Catholic kitchen of my childhood.

Indeed, Christianity was central to my upbringing. My hometown of Cork City had sprouted from a Christian settlement established by St Finbarr in 606 AD. (The name Finbarr *as Gaeilge* is Fionn Barr, which in English means 'fair head'.) First the church was built, then the school buildings and accommodation followed, along with a bakery and a brewery. Before you could say a quick decade of the rosary, a blacksmith, a shopkeeper and many other traders would have erected their place just outside the monastery wall.

Well-to-do families would send their sons to be educated, money flowed into the local economy and the settlement prospered. It was the same wherever monastic schools were established, and you can still identify them from the place names. Indeed, I was a seminarian myself. Yes, apart from my primary school years at the Christian Brothers North Monastery in Cork, I also spent two years at St Brendan's Seminary in Killarney. Incidentally, Killarney comes from the Irish Cill Airne, meaning 'church of blackthorn sloes'. St Brendan's Seminary was part of a large campus that included a boarding school, cathedral, Kerry Diocesan Offices, priests' accommodation, sports fields and more. Just like my hometown of Cork in the time of St Finbarr, the seminary in Killarney provided an education to the young men of the Kerry Diocese whose families could afford the fees. If they wanted their daughters to board, they were able to do so just over the high wall in the Presentation Convent. All this religious and scholarly activity saw the economy of these towns boom, both in Finbarr's time and in my day. As Pat Shortt and Jon Kenny of D'Unbelievables once said "Tiz good for de town, good for de parish".

THE AFRICAN ROOTS OF IRISH CHRISTIAN PLACE NAMES

It's interesting to note that some of Ireland's Christian place names may actually have their roots in Africa, as opposed to Rome, as you would think. I read of a very thought-provoking lecture delivered by Christianity expert Alf Monaghan, in which he explored the evidence that the Christianity movement in Ireland was instigated not by St Patrick, but in fact by the Coptic monks, who were escaping persecution in Egypt. Mr Monaghan pointed out in his lecture that a number of Irish place names boasted potential links to the Coptic monks, one of note being Donegal's Killybegs (Na Cealla Beaga, meaning 'little churches'). The patron saint of the parish of Killybegs is none other than St Catherine of Alexandria, Egypt.

There certainly appears to be considerable evidence backing the possibility that the Coptic monks introduced Christianity into Ireland. After all, St Patrick himself once expressed surprise at how many young boys and girls chose the monastic way of life, noting that the Irish had a predisposition for the contemplative life. Well, that we did … once! We must have got 'a taste for it' from the African Coptics before St Patrick got here. Perhaps they beat him to it!

CLONMACNOISE

Clonmacnoise/Cluain Mhic Nóis (meaning 'the meadow of the sons of Nós') is quite possibly the greatest Irish monastery of them all. Its location at the crossroads of Ireland, where the mighty Shannon is bisected by the ancient trackway that ran from west to east, was truly strategic. The passing traffic must have been considerable. When I last visited, underwater imagery revealed timber posts still rooted in the riverbed, suggesting a huge bridge once spanned the Shannon at this point. Even by today's standards, the scale of the site is staggering. The churches, a round tower, the dormitories, fields and associated infrastructure once supported a population of religious and lay people numbering up to two thousand. It was, in a manner of speaking, Ireland's very first city.

Clonmacnoise was a renowned spot, even many centuries ago. Travellers tended to overnight there on the great journey across the country. The Vikings, unfortunately, as a result of enjoying easy access up the broad River Shannon, were also aware of the settlement. They regularly raided Clonmacnoise, but then so too did the native Irish, and in time, the Normans also. There were rich pickings to be had there, and the site was relatively defenceless, so by the 12th century, Clonmacnoise began to decline, particularly as the fortified town of Athlone, a few miles upstream, offered a safer haven for the Clonmacnoise residents.

PLACES AND APOSTLES

Ireland's 12 apostles, as they're called, were all graduates of the monastic school of St Finian at Clonard/Cluain Eraird, meaning 'Eraird's meadow'. St Canice, the two St Brendans, the two St Ciarans and their fellow apostles all went out to spread 'the good news', and to this day, their names adorn cathedrals, seminaries, schools, churches, crossroads, holy wells, islands, football clubs, minor place names and street names.

ST CANICE OF AGHABOE (LAOIS)
Think you've never heard of St Canice? Think again! Kilkenny is named after him. Kilkenny comes from Cill Chainnigh, meaning 'church of Cainnech (or Canice)'.

ST BRENDAN OF CLONFERT (GALWAY)
Born near Tralee in County Kerry, he became known as St Brendan the Navigator, so it's no surprise to learn there is a church in Sicily named in his honour.

ST MOBHI OF GLASNEVIN (DUBLIN)
St Mobhi (Naomh Mobhí) lends his name to one of Dublin's finest thoroughfares, St Mobhi Road in Glasnevin.

ST CIARÁN OF SAIGHIR (OFFALY)
In California, you will find St Kieran's Catholic School, which was named in honour of our very own St Ciarán of Saighir.

ST CIARÁN OF CLONMACNOISE (OFFALY)

To this day, St Ciarán's association with Scotland remains strong. The town of Campbeltown, for instance, was actually originally known as Kinlochkilkerran, an anglicisation of the Gaelic for 'head of the loch by the kirk (church) of Ciarán'.

ST BRENDAN OF BIRR (OFFALY)

Known as St Brendan the Elder so as to distinguish him from fellow apostle St Brendan the Navigator, the exact location of his monastery in Birr has never been confirmed, although it is accepted by many to be situated on what is the current churchyard site of the Church of Ireland.

ST COLUMBA OF TERRYGLASS (TIPPERARY)

Sore head? Paracetamol not working? Get yourself to Tipp! In the village of Terryglass, you will find St Columba's Headache Well, which is said to cure headaches and migraines when you recite prayers and then wash your face and/or head in the water of the well.

ST RUADHÁN OF LORRHA (TIPPERARY)

St Ruadhán, famous for having placed a curse on the seat of Tara at one point, is said to be buried in a graveyard in Lorrha, however his exact burial place remains unknown, sadly.

ST SENÁN OF INISCATHAY (SCATTERY ISLAND, OFF THE COAST OF COUNTY CLARE)

While a number of Irish parishes and churches bear St Senán's name, it is interesting to note that many Irish families also carry it. The surname Gilsenan means 'devotees/followers of St Senán'. The surname Gilson also technically carries this meaning, as it is believed to have been an anglicisation of the name Gilsenan.

ST COLMCILLE/COLUMBA (ESTABLISHED MONASTERIES ACROSS IRELAND)

Donegal's Glencolmcille was named in honour of St Colmcille. It comes from Gleann Cholm Cille, meaning 'valley of Colm Cille'.

ST NINNIDH OF LOUGH ERNE (FERMANAGH)

The Fermanagh village of Knockninny gets its name from St Ninnidh, who has long been associated with Lough Erne.

ST MOLAISE OF DEVENISH ISLAND (FERMANAGH)

Also known as Laisrén mac Nad Froích, St Molaise is said to have established his monastery on Devenish Island while on the pilgrim route to Croagh Patrick in County Mayo.

- -

GLASNEVIN, COUNTY DUBLIN
Glasnevin – Glas Naíon
Glas – Stream
Naoín – Infant
Glas Naíon therefore means 'stream of the infant'.

SAINTS AND SCHOLARS

As the fire of Christianity and learning took hold and spread through the island of Ireland, we produced saints and scholars by the thousand. A huge portion of the Irish population was now teaching, studying or working in and around our monastic settlements. More and more Irish were leaving Ireland and spreading the gospel and education abroad. St Columba, for instance, is credited with converting the Picts of Scotland. Following the fall of the Roman Empire, Irish religious orders set up colleges of learning across Europe – places like the Irish College in Paris, the Irish Franciscan

College St Anthony's in Louvain, Belgium, the Irish College of St Patrick at Douai, France, and the Irish College at Lisbon, Portugal. These are just a few! They left their mark all over Europe in terms of place names also. There's Patricks Fjord in Iceland and the generic place name 'Bridewell', which, in Irish, is Tobar Bhríde, reflecting its deep roots in the holy water of Ireland's St Bridget.

THE SAINTS IN THE PLACE NAMES

St Oliver Plunkett Parish, Pennsylvania, USA

Brigantia (St Bridget), Yorkshire, England

Saint Patrick's Village, Missouri, USA

Inchcolm (St Columba's Island), Scotland

St Oliver Plunkett Parish, New South Wales, Australia

Kilbrandon (St Brendan), Scotland

Bridekirk (St Bridget), Cumbria, England

Barra Isle (St Finbarr), Scotland

I can understand how the Christian Gospel, or 'The Good News' of forgiveness and of a father figure in heaven who loves us all, particularly the sinner, might have gained traction here. Although a sophisticated society, the pre-Christian Irish still engaged in practices like human sacrifice. I remember Professor Ned Kelly of the National Museum of Ireland taking me to the bogs of County Offaly to show me the very spot where he discovered the mutilated body of an ancient king, now known as 'Croghan Man'. His remarkably well-preserved remains are still on view at the National Museum of Ireland. Professor Ned explained that, on foot of some plague or pestilence that 'Croghan Man', as king, had failed to avert, he had been tied up, mutilated, nipples removed with a knife and his bound body buried in a bog. Modern-day Irish politics can be tough, but the price of poor leadership in the pre-Christian era was not for the faint-hearted.

The Christian message, when it came, must have seemed particularly benign. I read one account of the life of St Patrick, where he was described as a fearless man who, amongst other things, 'refused to take mead before sleep'. In a land of mythology, serpents, human sacrifice and long dark nights, you can see how folk around Slane and Tara might have considered St Patrick 'a hardy buck, right enough'.

Despite the mass conversion of Ireland by Patrick and others, I still smile to myself whenever I hear callers to radio phone-in shows trot out the old cliché.

'Well, as a Christian country, Ireland …'

Christian country? I suppose it depends on what you mean by 'Christian'. Apart from anything else, recent stats for religious observance would suggest that Irish society now has numerous citizens of other faiths and a considerable number of people who would describe themselves as 'none of the above'.

However, if you were to take a bird's-eye view of the place-names map of Ireland, you'd have to say, 'it looks pretty Christian from up here!'

The Irish words for monastery (*mainistir*), church (*cill*), diocese (*na déise*), convent (*clochar*), saint (*naomh*) and even the devil (*an diabhal*) pepper the map.

SPEAK OF THE DEVIL!

The devil appears in many place names, the most famous being Devilsbit Mountain in County Tipperary. When a mountain has a name like Devilsbit, you just know the story behind it is going to be decent. Well, as it turns out, there's more than one story, but they all seem to involve the creation of the Rock of Cashel. One account claims that the devil took a bite out of a mountain in a bid to throw the rock at St Patrick but instead it landed in Cashel, giving us what is now known as the Rock of Cashel, and leaving us with a mountain now known as Devilsbit (Bearnán Éile).

Another legend maintains that when the devil took a bite from the mountain, he broke a tooth and immediately spat it out. The tooth landed in Cashel, and there you have another explanation of how the Rock of Cashel was formed. I'm inclined to go with the latter. From the old Cork–Dublin road it looks exactly like a giant molar! It's worth noting that the Rock of Cashel is also known as 'St Patrick's Rock', as it was there our patron saint is said to have baptised King Aengus, who in turn became the country's first Christian ruler. In terms of there being a grain of truth in mythology, I could see how the rock on the plain of Tipperary would fit neatly into Devilsbit, from which it was cast out, not by the devil, I suspect, but by a glacier! However, rock samples from both locations show there's no match.

The shift from pagan to Christian was not without compromise. Many of our pre-Christian rites, rituals and festivals continued with just a minor tweak. Pagan mid-winter festivals, for instance, became Christmas. The practice of bringing holly and ivy into the house at Christmas was originally a druidic custom. These evergreen plants that survive winter were a pre-Christian symbol of the continuity of life through the die-back period of winter. Similarly, the custom of the mistletoe at New Year also draws on druidic tradition. The revered yew tree was at this point also being incorporated into

Christian burial sites. Pre-Christian deities were ascribed Christian names; so too were rivers and place names. To this day, the pagan magic lives. Some of our finest towns, racecourses and farms have fairies, ghosts and druidic magic lying dormant just beneath the sod, so before you build a bungalow or begin digging the foundations for a new development, you might be well advised to stall the digger and get out the place-names map! For example:

▷ Druid's Altar (Cloch an Draoi)/Drombeg, County Cork

▷ Carricknabishoge Point (Carraig na bPiseog, meaning 'the rock of the curses'), Aran Island of Inis Mór, County Galway

▷ Ballynashee (Baile na Sí, meaning 'fairies' town'), County Sligo

▷ Fairyhouse (Tigh na Sióg, meaning 'house of the fairies'), County Meath

▷ Banshee (Binn Sí, meaning 'peak of the fairies'), County Dublin

▷ Tyshe River (Abhainn na Taibhse, meaning 'river of ghosts'), County Kerry

▷ Cuan na Spride (meaning 'harbour of the ghost'), County Limerick

▷ Owenpollaphuca (Abhainn Pholl an Phúca, meaning 'river of the hole of the Púca' (i.e. the Pooka or rogue fairy), County Mayo

▷ Newry (An tIúr, meaning 'the yew tree'), County Down

▷ Mayo (Maigh Eo, meaning 'plain of the yew tree')

Most great cultural changes come slowly at first, but from the fifth century onwards, Christianity spread rapidly across the land, and references increasingly appear in our *logainmneacha* and when naming children at baptism, or 'christening', as it's called. I was given the Christian name John after Pope John XXIII, who died in the days before my arrival. The two events were not connected, but my father maintained, 'There wouldn't be room enough on the planet for two of ye!'

The term 'Christian name' has been replaced by the more internationally recognised term 'first name'. Nowadays, when filling in a form, you will be asked to provide your 'first name' and 'family name', but old habits die hard, and I got a right quare look in the rear-view mirror recently when I asked a Sikh taxi driver displaying the taxi ID Gulshandeep Singh, how he pronounced his Christian name! He replied 'Paddy'. Amidst the chuckles, I enquired if his Sikh first name could be translated and he explained that Gulshandeep means 'the lamp of the rose garden'. Nice, but I reckon my papal connection trumps even that!

As Christian zeal swept the land, it seems that everything that could be named was given a Christian name. Indeed, much of Ireland's flora and fauna were also 'branded' Christian, in a most delightful way. The humble little ladybird is called *bóín Dé*, meaning 'God's little cow', and the beautiful drooping fuchsia blossoms that fill our hedgerows are named *deora Dé*, meaning 'God's tears'.

MONASTIC SETTLEMENTS EVOLVE INTO TOWNS AND CITIES

Monasticism has its origins in North Africa. It demands withdrawal from the secular life and replacing it with a life of quiet reflection and strict adherence to 'the monastic rule', whilst living in a community of monks or sisters, as the case may be.

The monastic rule of St Ailbe of Emly was written in Old Irish and sets out the standards by which a monk must live his life. It instructs the monk to speak little, have a tender conscience, work hard, serve the sick and deal gently with sinners, and to be wise, learned, pious, generous, courteous and modest in dress.

The traditional name ascribed to a nun was *cailleach*. The same word also means 'divine hag', 'a veiled woman', 'a crone'. Interestingly, the Irish word *caille* means 'hood' or 'veil', so it's easy to see why the term might be a root of the word to describe a nun.

Ireland has a multitude of place names with religious references, many of which you may not be aware of. Limerick's Holycross would be a pretty obvious one, but Baile na gCailleach may not. The name directly translates as 'town of the nuns'. Each of the following comes from the same Irish name (Baile na gCailleach):

▷ Collinstown, County Westmeath

▷ Ballynagale, County Wexford

▷ Calliaghstown, County Dublin

▷ Collierstown, County Meath

▷ Callystown,County Louth

▷ Ballynagalliagh, County Sligo

▷ Ballynagally, County Limerick

▷ Calliaghstown, County Meath

▷ Ballynagalliagh, County Kildare

▷ Holycross, County Limerick

▷ Collierstown, County Meath

▷ Galliagh, County Derry

SAINT KEVIN AND THE HOLLYWOOD CONNECTION!

It seems the origins of America's most famous place name may actually be found in Irish soil! As some of you may know, there already exists a village in County Wicklow called Hollywood, and while it has been argued that the village was named after the number of holly trees in the area, there is another very strong debate that suggests it was originally called Holy Wood because of St Kevin's presence there. Over time, however, Holy Wood became known as Hollywood, and so was born the place name we have today. It's not unusual. I've come across many places called Hollywell, that clearly began as 'Holy Well'. As for America's Hollywood, however, it seems a Wicklow man by the name of Matthew Guirke was responsible for naming the now famous showbiz neighbourhood. During the Famine, Matthew emigrated to California, where he spent a number of years acquiring new skills and establishing himself as a businessman. Having built a cabin in a Californian suburb, he decided to name his new home in honour of his original home in Wicklow – Hollywood. That simple! So the next time you see a picture of that famous sign up in the Santa Monica Hills, spare a thought for the two Irishmen responsible for it: St Kevin and Matthew Guirke.

Given the strength of St Kevin's association with Hollywood (the Wicklow one!), you may be wondering why his connection with Glendalough is so much stronger? Why didn't he construct his round tower in Hollywood? Well, it seems Kevin had to leave Hollywood as a result of being constantly pursued by an infatuated local woman called Kathleen. According to legend, when Kathleen followed him into the woods one day, Kevin threw himself into a bed of nettles to hide from her, or perhaps to purge his lust. Fed up with her unrelenting advances (and the nettle stings no doubt!), Kevin eventually fled Hollywood for the complete isolation of Glendalough ('the glen with the two lakes'), where his followers went on to build the famous round tower.

MOUNT MELLERAY

In the summer of 2016, I spent a few days on retreat in the Cistercian monastery of Mount Melleray in the Knockmealdown Mountains (Cnoc Mhaoldomhnaigh meaning 'Muldowney's mountain'), in County Waterford. I'd heard that a little monasticism can be good for you, but in keeping with the monastic principle of 'all things in moderation', I decided to take the 'penance light' option and booked in for just two days. This enclosed order of Trappists lives according to the 'Rule of Benedict' and keeps a vow of silence.

Housemaster Father Denis-Luke is charged with tending to guests, and so is permitted to speak. He welcomed me warmly and even offered to carry my rucksack, which I declined, as he ushered me through the faded splendour of a once bustling monastery. Father Denis-Luke is a man in his 70s, balding, with glasses, and I'd say he was tall once. He led me up the bare stairs, issuing blessings and welcomes with virtually every step, assuring me that he was delighted to meet me. Father Denis-Luke explained that Mount Melleray Abbey was the first monastery to open in 1832 following Catholic emancipation. Almost three hundred years had elapsed since the monastic light had been quenched by Cromwell and the dissolution of the monasteries.

'People were delighted to have the monasteries back,' he told me, 'but sure little did the poor craturs know that the Famine was only a few years around the corner.'

He showed me to my room, with its locker, coat hanger, alarm clock and a single bed. They don't do double rooms in Mount Melleray.

'I don't expect you will have much energy for reading after your long trip, but you're welcome to this copy of *The Rule of Saint Benedict*.' He handed me a small red book of about 60 pages, and once he was sure I needed nothing to eat, he was gone out of the door with a 'God bless. Sleep well.'

I set my alarm clock for 3.30am, then I set my phone alarm for 3.50am, 5.45am and 7am. The seven monks and three house guests rose several times during the night to pray. Vigils are at 4.20am, when the brotherhood immerses itself in the chanting of psalms, as if they were keeping vigil with Christ in the Garden of Gethsemane. Then, two hours later, they gather again for Lauds, from the Latin word for 'praise', which is also the point where the community greets the rising sun as a symbol of the resurrection. Mass is at 7.30am. Each time, the monks entered and exited the church through their own door, and not a word was exchanged between us.

That didn't stop their house guests from chatting. After a simple breakfast of porridge, sliced pan, a banana and tea, we washed our dishes by hand. A fellow guest who told me he had been coming here for years volunteered his story.

'Gambling and drink,' he said. 'I'd come up here to "dry out" twice a year, and I was never once asked why. That went on for years. When I was ready, I asked for an ear and an old shoulder to cry on. Jesus, once I started, I didn't stop bawlin' for a day and a half. I still come up twice a year, but I pay my way now,' he said, smiling with the lightness of a man set free as he scraped porridge off a huge serving spoon.

I was in the chapel thinking about the comfort of an old shoulder when Father Denis-Luke arrived and showed me a cavernous vaulted room behind the altar. This room was as big as many churches I've seen. There were a few work benches, some tools at one end, and around two of the walls were a series of sinks in various states of disrepair, some of them literally hanging by a few rusty bolts. We found two broken chairs and sat to talk. When I asked about the four boxes of books in the middle of the floor, he explained that each of the boxes housed the contents of a room.

'They'd be the last four men to die here. Ah sure, I knew them all well. I'll have to give their few things to a charity when we get a chance. They're only gathering dust.'

'That man there.' He nodded towards a cardboard box with Fyffes bananas printed on the side. 'He was a brilliant man. He could read sacred text in several languages. Sure, that's mostly what's in the box, but it's hard to let go of them, when his name is on them. But I will now, when I get organised.'

'And all the sinks?' I enquired. 'What are they for?'

'Ah well, y'see, this was once the sacristy, John,' he explained. 'I can remember mornings when over a hundred priests in their vestments would be in here, washing their faces and hands in those sinks before joining the queue for an available altar to say Mass.'

It was going-home time, so I collected my bag and popped down to the kitchen to say goodbye.

When I thanked him for his kindness, Father Denis-Luke explained, 'Hospitality has always been regarded as a golden rule. No one is to be turned away, no questions are to be asked and no payment sought. St Benedict instructs us all that the stranger at the door should be welcomed as though it were Christ himself.'

'I wonder if that's where we got our international reputation for the *céad míle fáilte*?'

'I don't know anything about that,' he replied. 'But I'd better go up and collect Brother Bernard's tray.'

We shook hands and I haven't seen the man since.

On the slow drive home from Mount Melleray, my mind wandered back down *bóithrín na smaointe*. I thought about Denis-Luke and his old friend with all his earthly goods in a banana box. I considered the value of an old shoulder to cry on and the symbolism of the serving spoon. As my car negotiated the country roads back through Midleton (whose Irish name is Mainistir na

Corran, meaning 'the monastery at the weir'), and on home to Cork City, itself rooted in a monastic settlement, I considered the huge part of Irish history occupied by these gentle men and women. I thought about their dwindling numbers and the reputation they earned for Ireland as the 'Land of Saints and Scholars'. Irish teachers and Irish schools are still highly regarded around the world. Above all else, I was struck by the unqualified welcome that still awaits the stranger 'as though it were Christ himself at the door'. I had come to understand that 'Ireland of the Welcomes' is more than just a brand.

AHAMORE ABBEY, COUNTY KERRY
Ahamore Abbey – Mainistir Achaidh Mhóir
Mainistir – Monastery
Achadh (Achaidh) – Field
Mór (Mhóir) – Big/Large
Ahamore Abbey therefore means 'the monastery of the big field'.

GRAIGUENAMANAGH, COUNTY KILKENNY
Graiguenamanagh – Gráig na Manach
Gráig – Hamlet/settlement
Na Manach – of the Monks
Graiguenamanagh therefore means 'hamlet/settlement of the monks'.

MONASTERBOICE, COUNTY LOUTH
Monasterboice – Mainistir Bhuithe
Mainistir – Monastery
Buithe – St Boethius
Monasterboice therefore means 'Boethius's monastery'.

KNOCKVICAR, ROSCOMMON
Knockvicar – Cnoc an Bhiocáire
Cnoc – Hill
Biocáire (Bhiocáire) – Vicar
Knockvicar therefore means 'the vicar's hill'.

KILRONAN, INIS MÓR, ARAN ISLANDS
Kilronan – Cill Rónáin
Cill – Church
Rónán (Rónáin) – Ronan
Kilronan therefore means 'Ronan's church'.

KILLYMAN, COUNTY TYRONE
Killyman – Cill na mBan
Cill – Church
Na mBan – of the Women
Killyman therefore means 'church of the women'.

Those of us who were educated in the seminaries, convents and monasteries of Ireland, myself included, will have mixed tales to tell, particularly of the harsher regimes that took hold of so many Irish institutions run by religious orders. It certainly hastened their demise. I expect monasticism, just like communism, Catholicism and most other 'isms', began with the full gale of righteousness and good intentions, but became rigid, brittle and ultimately foundered on the rocks of self-righteousness. Like many great ideals, Irish monasticism has receded. In recent years a small number of Buddhist and Christian retreats have sprouted in the wild places of Ireland. Perhaps here monasticism has found a crevice where the principles of contemplation, learning, service and hospitality will take root and blossom again as we enter the post-pandemic chapter of human development.

One thing is certain, however: despite their vow of silence, the Irish brothers and sisters of old certainly left more than their fair share of words in the great books of Europe and their names scattered across the place-names map of the world.

5

THE VIKINGS

'Quick! *Brostaigí!* Run! They're coming!'

When we Irish flee, we usually do our fleeing westwards, looking back over our shoulders as another foreign force enters from 'stage east'. Over the centuries, there have been quite a few outsiders who decided they'd like a little of our action. Gold? Land? Slaves? We got 'em all! We've had numerous waves of fighting men land on Irish shores, and they nearly always approached from the east. The good guys, like the French and the Spanish, usually came round by the back door and were heartily welcomed by the native Irish as we tried again and again to restore our Gaelic civilisation.

However, wave after wave of trouble has crashed onto our eastern shores, each tide leaving its own mark on the history, place names and family names of Ireland. The most notorious and, dare I say, romanticised of them all is the Viking. Even the word itself, 'Viking', looks impressive in print. Solid letters, with sharp angles. Like the word 'Nazi', it proclaims terror. No, there's nothing soft about the word 'Viking'. It originated from *víkingr*, meaning 'a sea adventurer' in Old Norse.

As I discovered from Poll Moussoulides, my voice-coach on the set of the TV series *Vikings*, there's a clipped sound to Old Norse. So just like a monk watching the landscape for raiders from the top of a round tower, you too must listen very carefully as you scan the map for any sign of Vikings. Listen to the sound of the words. Sometimes you'll hear something unusual. Scanning the south coast of Ireland, all seems well and everything in its place, but then you spot the place name Helvick! Like a monk reacting to the sharp crack of a snapping twig, the toponymist also twigs, 'Helvick? Aha! Viking!'

- -
HELVICK HEAD, WATERFORD
Helvick Head in Irish is Ceann Heilbhic, deriving from the Old Norse hellavík, meaning 'bright bay', or helgavík, meaning 'safe bay'.

Y'see, when you're Viking hunting, you need to know where they are most likely to be hiding, and you need to recognise one when you see one. I'm only an amateur place-name hunter, but my enquiries keep bringing me back to the same kinds of places. Yes, the kinda places where I can almost smell a Viking. Well, you know what I mean … the coasts and waterways of Ireland.

The first Viking raid on Ireland took place in 795 AD, when these Scandinavian sea-warriors set their sights on Rathlin Island, just off the north-east coast. That same year, the islands of Inishbofin off the coast of County Galway and Inishmurray off the coast of County Sligo also found themselves at the centre of Viking raids. Clearly, Ireland held considerable appeal for our Scandinavian visitors, particularly in terms of sustenance, as the Annals of the Four Masters reveal that, by the year 841, many Vikings were choosing to spend the cold winter months here.

Whenever the Vikings were on their travels, they would temporarily moor their ships in what were known as 'longphorts' (later spelled 'longfort'). The longphort would become their base for the duration of their stay in an area. Some of these temporary bases, which were used for trading as well as raiding, became settlements and actual towns in their own right. Places like Dublin, Waterford, Wexford and Cork all developed as trading hubs thanks to the Vikings choosing to moor their boats in the longphorts they had established there. Of course, as the Vikings began to explore our major rivers and travel further inland, their influence permeated some of our midland counties.

Apart from the random smash and grab raids, they also traded goods with the native Irish, but when they raided the Kilkenny townland of Dunmore in AD 928, it was by far their most wicked act of cruelty. Simply put, it was a massacre. As documented in the Annals of the Four Masters, when the raiders struck, local people fled to the safety of Dunmore Cave, where they had hoped to hide until the foreign invaders left. Unfortunately, fate had other plans and, before long, they were located. The Vikings had decided to apprehend those in hiding with a view to selling them on as slaves; however, in order to capture them, they would have to force them out from the cave. To do this, they decided to light fires at the mouth of the cave in the hope that the smoke would eventually leave those inside with no choice but to abandon their shelter. As the fires raged, however, all the oxygen inside the cave was absorbed and over a thousand people perished.

In the early 1970s, skeletal remains were discovered inside the cave, while in 1999, a variety of silver and copper items – believed to have originally been hidden there by the Vikings – were discovered within a cleft inside the cave. Sometimes when we look back on history, figures like the Vikings almost seem fictional. We often forget that they actually existed and struck real terror into the hearts of the native Irish. However, as you descend the steps, into the cavernous limestone Dunmore cave almost 50 metres below the surface, the reality of what actually happened to those women, men and children starts to hit home. In fact, if you stay really still, you will sometimes hear creaking sounds emanate from the narrow spaces at the back of the chamber where people once trembled …

FROM MEGENLAND TO MAINLAND

In 2009, RTÉ had me visit the Shetland Islands to film a report for the travel show *No Frontiers*. Shetland boasts, amongst other tourist attractions, Britain's most northerly post office. Yes, seriously, it's in all the tourist brochures. Although governed from Westminster and the Scottish Parliament, where it shares one MP with the Orkney Islands, this archipelago of islands sounds and feels more like Scandinavia.

There's scarcely a set of bagpipes to be seen. Instead, the musical weapon of choice is the Hardanger fiddle. I attended a fiddle festival on the largest of the islands, curiously named 'Mainland', even though it's out in the middle of nowhere, where the Atlantic Ocean meets the North Sea. Anyway, Shetland was a perfect refuelling pit stop for the Vikings on their long journeys south. The DNA of islanders would suggest there was even the occasional overnight stay.

'So what about your place names?' I enquired of wildlife ranger Brydon Thompson, as we went in search of puffin colonies out on the cliffs. 'I mean, what about your island names, Unst and Yell. They sound like a huge PA system at a rave! Where did they come from? Vikings, I suppose?'

'No one's quite sure,' Brydon explained. 'They seem to sound like Old Norse, particularly Yell, which sounds very like the old Viking word *jála* [pronounced 'yall', and meaning 'barren'], so it's a possible match, but many scholars expect that these are probably Pictish words. The Picts lived all over Scotland and the isles.'

'So what about your biggest island, Mainland? That's English, I expect?'

'Well, it's English now, but it most likely evolved from "Megenland", the Viking term for, well, "mainland"!'

'Right, and the capital, Lerwick?' I asked. 'Sounds like Berwick, as in Berwick-upon-Tweed. That's ever so British, right?'

'Wrong again, John.' Brydon smiled. 'It began as "Leirvik". It's a mixture of Old Norse and Norn, a language once spoken locally. It translates as "bay of clay". In Old Norse, *ler* means "clay", and *wick* means "inlet" or "bay".'

Indeed, I found many other Lerwicks in Norway, and also on the Faroe Islands. All good Viking territories. They're two a penny, like Ballybegs in Ireland.

All across the north-eastern corner of Europe, the suffix -*wick* is a good sign the Vikings have landed. Now we're really on to something here. At home in Ireland, I discovered we have a couple of 'wicks' that tell the tale, including Smerwick Harbour in the West Kerry Gaeltacht, derived from *smjor-vik*, meaning 'butter bay'. Some toponymists have put forward differing opinions, but given the location of Smerwick, I can easily visualise a longship pulling in for supplies. Furthermore, the Vikings' *grá* for butter was a match for our own. Then there's also the aforementioned 'Helvick' on the Waterford coast, as well as Reykjavík, the capital of Iceland, which means 'bay of smokes'. So named, I thought, because as you approached the coastline from the sea, you could get a fix on where your mates were camped from the wisps of black smoke against the white nothingness of winter. Brilliant! Except no, apparently not.

When I was up there for a football match between Valur and Cork City FC in 2004, a local schoolteacher in the stand explained to me that 'the smokes' in Reykjavík were the puffs of steam from the geysers. Aha! Incidentally, Iceland, or Ísland, as it's called in Icelandic, was unpopulated until the Vikings arrived and began using it as a base. Given that many of them are said to have taken wives and slaves when raiding Ireland and Scotland, it's no wonder that recent studies have shown a significant presence of Gaelic DNA in the Icelandic population of today. Looks-wise, there is at times a striking similarity between women of an Icelandic origin and those who are Irish or Scottish. Red hair and pale skin are classic traits we associate with all three places!

Just as the Mountains of Mourne sweep down to the sea and the fjords of Norway sweep up to the sky, the word *fjord* swept into Ireland in the Viking's wake. Some of Ireland's finest place names still feature this term. Take Wexford, from *veisa-fjordr*, meaning 'muddy ford'. They certainly got that one right! To this day, Wexford is famous for the Wexford Slobs, a remarkable haven for wetland birds. A shallow place to pull your longship ashore, restock with fresh water, fish and wild fowl – this is Viking heaven!

Similarly, we have:

▷ County Louth's Carlingford, situated on the Cooley Peninsula, is one of the most beautiful settings on this island. Can you hear any trace of Viking in Carlingford? Yes, there it is again, *kerling-fjordr*, meaning 'old woman fjord'. When you work out why it's 'old woman', please let me know!

▷ Nearby, Strangford, the 'handle of Ireland' as I see it, that long narrow peninsula that curves southwards behind Belfast on the north-east coast, is an easier code to crack. Strangford from *strangr fjordr* simply means 'strong fjord'. Elementary, my dear Watson!

▷ Waterford is synonymous with the Vikings, but did you know that its very name has Viking origins? The Norse translation of 'Waterford' is *veora-fjoror*, meaning 'ram fjord'.

VIKING IMPACT ON IRISH NAMES

One of the Irish words for a Viking is *Lochlannach*, and that term has since entered the Irish lexicon as the boy's name Lochlann. The surnames MacLochlainn and O'Loughlin similarly both mean 'son of the Viking'. What I found very interesting are the commonplace Irish surnames that boast Viking origins.

▷ Higgins – The surname of our president is actually the anglicisation of Ó hUiginn, which itself is derived from the Irish word *uiginn* meaning 'Viking'. Those with the surname Higgins are in fact believed to be descended from Niall of the Nine Hostages.

▷ Reynolds – This is a derivative of the Old Norse word *rögnvaldr*, which is composed of the words *ragina*, meaning 'advice/counsel' and *waldaz*, meaning 'ruler/sovereign'.

▷ Doyle – The good old Irish surname Doyle is believed to have Norse roots. Converted to Irish, it translates as Ó Dubhghaill, meaning 'the dark stranger/foreigner', a fairly frank term used by the Irish in describing the Vikings.

▷ Cotter – This surname is of Norse-Gaelic origin, but this really only becomes evident in its Irish form, 'Mac Oitir'. Oitir is in fact a derivative of the Viking name Ottarr, which is composed of the words *otti*, meaning 'fear', and *herr*, meaning 'army'.

There are some truly beautiful names in Ireland thanks to the Vikings. Take for example the traditional singer Muireann Nic Amhlaoibh. Muireann is from Corca Dhuibhne in Kerry and an Irish speaker, as her name suggests. However, if you were to translate it into English, it would be Muireann McAuliffe. Drill down into its roots and what is revealed is a deep Scandinavian connection. The name 'Muireann' literally means 'the fair sea woman'. In fact, according to the Annals, Muireann was a mermaid turned back into a woman by an early Christian saint, Comgall. The word 'nic', meanwhile, translates as 'daughter of', while the last part of her name, 'Amhlaoibh', is the genitive of Olaf, a popular man's name in Scandinavian countries.

Combine the lot together and what picture does it paint? A fair-haired sea woman, daughter of Olaf the Viking. Now, I ask you, is there a more romantic name for a female singer from the shores of the Atlantic?

Lasairfhíona Ní Chonaola, another singer I know, hails from the Aran Island of Inis Oírr (meaning 'the easterly island') and her name also holds behind it a beautiful meaning. 'Lasairfhíona' directly translates as 'a glint of light in a glass of wine'. I find it beautiful that two of my favourite singers have such imagery in their names.

THE CRAIC IN THE CODE

It would be hard to describe *Dindsenchas*, the lore of places, or even toponymy, as an exact science. Often it's like trying to read a well-weathered headstone. If you can see that a person was buried in 1789, but the first two numbers are eroded to the point of being illegible – born … 29, died 1789 – well, you can probably take it that the first two numbers were also '17', and that the poor man was 60 when he died, rather than, say, 160. Clearly, you can follow up the rest of the man's story by starting with the parish records, but quite often the combination of time, misspelling, mispronunciation, bad translation and change of land ownership will see a *logainm* morph so much that we don't know whether our ancestors were describing a church/*cill* or a wood/*coill*. Local records, historians, folklorists, postmen and shopkeepers can all help in the untangling of a place name, but there are still plenty of place-name puzzles that do not have a definitive answer. This suits me just fine, given my love of 'speculation and investigation' as I travel the roads of Ireland with my pocket *foclóir* in the glovebox of my car.

I remember when the latest version of the county car-registration plates first came into being in 1991, I was tootling along behind a car with the new Longford reg.

'LD? Yeah, that makes perfect sense.'

As I squinted to establish the Irish translation written above the LD, however, I thought, 'Ah no, surely Longford is an English name?'

It reads like English, 'Long Ford'. The name is exactly what it says on the tin. It's a shallow crossing of the river. That's why it's called 'Longford' in English, but a 'long ford' in the original Irish language would be given as *áth fada*. So, if it were anglicised, while remaining true to its original name, then the place should probably have been called 'Afaddy'. Why would they go and bend two English words to sound like some Irish peasant trying to pronounce an English name and give Longford in Irish as Longfort? Alas! I was wrong. Completely wrong, in fact!

As I mentioned earlier in the chapter, while the Vikings were away on their adventures, they would use temporary moorings to restock the food and fresh water on board. This was referred to as a 'longphort' from the Old Norse words *long*, meaning 'ship', and *port*, meaning 'mooring'. Longford, like many Irish towns, grew out of one of these temporary bases. So, I give you the modern-day town of LD! Or, as it was originally called, and is still correctly called in Irish, An Longfort. So, whenever you see a townland on a map called 'Longford', and there are a few, remember it has nothing to do with a broad river crossing – more likely it reads as some ancient graffiti saying 'We wuz 'ere, signed the Vikings'!

Incidentally, the river upon which the town of Longford evolved is a tributary of the River Shannon called the Camlin, from the Irish words *cam*, meaning 'crooked', and *linn*, meaning 'pool'. Armed with the above knowledge and, without the use of my trusty *foclóir*, I found myself at the centre of a heated debate in a Limerick pub about the origins of the local Athlunkard Street.

'They were merchants,' said the barman.

'Not at all,' said the man by the fire, sounding like an authority who had pounded the pavements of Limerick more than anyone else in the bar. 'The Athlunkards came from France away back. Sure they owned half the city at one stage.'

Having considered the conundrum for a while, I was keen to offer my own tuppence worth. As a blow-in, I should probably have kept my mouth shut. My Cork accent, not to mind my theory I was about to proffer on the Athlunkards, could have been enough to stir up some old battle from the hurling pitches of Munster.

'Sorry,' I ventured, 'just thinking here. If you break up the word you get "Ath" at the beginning. That's the Irish word for a ford or a stretch of shallow water. I wonder, is there any chance that "Lunkard" evolved from "longphort" the old Viking term for a mooring?'

That such presumption should emanate from a Corkman took the bar by surprise. There was a momentary silence before the barman had the wisdom to look it up on the Internet.

'I have it!' he declared. 'Athlunkard Street, Limerick, from the Irish Sráid Áth Longphoirt, meaning "the street of the ford of the Viking camp".'

Rather than having to reverse red-faced out of the pub, praising Limerick's glorious past and apologising for my ignorance, I found myself staying on. The lad by the fire even bought me a pint.

A hit! Indeed there will be many hits and misses when trying to crack the code of Irish place names. I call it the 'craic in the code'. Enjoy it!

ÓL AND CEOL WITH THE 'VÍKINGR GANG'

Many years ago, when travelling through Scandinavia, I was taken aback when, every now and then, I heard conversations include a word that sounded just like an old friend from home. Entering a Calvinist church in Denmark for a snoop around, I reached for the door handle, and the brass plate that would normally read 'Push' at home, here read 'Traekke'. I did just that. I pushed really hard, but to no avail. Eventually, a kind woman explained to me that the sign actually means 'pull', not 'push', and that the word *traekke* is pronounced 'dragge' in Danish and 'draw' in both Swedish and Norwegian. Right, so up here, 'drag' or 'draw' means 'pull'. That sounds remarkably like home. I retired for an *øl* (a beer) and traded words common to both cultures with the barman.

'Y'know, my local back in Ireland also has a sign that reads "Ól", meaning "beer". In fact, it says "Ól, Ceol agus Craic".'

'Yes, we have given you guys so many words in English, like "daughter" and "slaughter" plus a few Viking tough words like "anger" (from *angr*), "berserk" (from *berserkr*), as well as "gang" meaning a group of men.'

I discovered the Scandinavian roots of everyday English words like 'haggle' and 'husband' and 'gift' (originally meaning a dowry). Even 'ombudsman' is an Old Norse term meaning 'steward' or 'commissioner', from *umbodsmadr*.

The barman was chuffed when I told him that not only had his predecessors influenced the English language, but they had also left some of their finest words in the Irish language, like *bád/bát*, meaning 'boat', and *ispín*, meaning 'sausage'. I explained that these stray words have found good homes in Ireland, where they are still in daily use in the *Gaeltachtaí*.

At the end of an illuminating night of swapping words and rounds of beer, I was beginning to relate to ye olde Dubliner, *ag ól* with the Víkingr gang after a tough day haggling about payment for drawing ropes and dragging longships to the quay wall. Y'see, that's the thing about the Vikings. They weren't all bad. Okay, they've had a lot of bad press over the years, but so too have the 'fighting Irish'. Let's face it, nearly every race has been partial to a bit of plundering and pillaging somewhere along the way.

Although the Vikings carried out lightning raids on easily accessed Irish communities, they had no ambition to colonise the island of Ireland, unlike some of those who came after them. For an empire to thrive, it has to crush the local culture and rob the people of their language, their religious beliefs, their identity. We've seen this methodology employed by the Romans, the Conquistadors of South America, the British Empire and many more. The age-old message to the native was clear, 'You must become a second class "us".' However, the Scandinavians displayed little interest in changing us; they merely wanted to rob us and, for that, I'd like to publicly thank them.

This 'visitor visa' approach is reflected in the light footprint they left behind. They didn't build castles and they weren't interested in administering a foreign colony. No, they were in and out like a smash 'n' grab raid, and Irish monasteries provided rich pickings. Eventually, the longphorts established for these raids became more permanent features. Before you could say 'Come in, Sigfrid, your smorgasbord is ready,' they were beginning to assimilate and marry. It was at this point that their names entered Irish culture.

Virtually all of our Viking place names are coastal. Picture it, a longship full of thirsty Vikings heading down the Irish Sea, trying to navigate without a satnav or local knowledge. It can't have been easy, so the Norsemen had to make a note of the islands, distinctive rocks and headlands as they went. Clearly, they had to name them for easy reference on future tours. I can just imagine an ancestor of Christy Moore strumming a lute at the back of the boat and singing, 'Is it right or left for Gibraltar?' Or even, 'The Craic was Ninety on the Isle of Man'!

As they launched raids from their bases in Scandinavia and along the British coastline, they dropped their words like confetti at a wedding. A great example would be one of their most commonly used words, *ey*. This was their word for 'island', and it pops up all along this Viking superhighway on our coast.

Here are some prime examples:

▷ Dursey, from *djorrs-ey*, meaning 'bull island'.

▷ Lambay, from *lamb-ey*, meaning 'lamb island'.

▷ Saltees, from *salt-ey*, meaning 'salt island'.

▷ Dalkey, from *dalk-eyja*, meaning 'thorn island'.

And then there's the one that always puzzled me as a child: Ireland's Eye. It turns out it's derived from *Erin's-ey*, meaning 'Ireland's Island'. It's the Viking equivalent of 'You've arrived !'

Then of course there is Fastnet Rock, a fairly unusual name. Ever wondered about that one? Yep, Viking. It comes from *hvastann-ey*, meaning 'sharp-toothed island'. A brilliant description. I've been out there filming with the lighthouse attendants, and that's exactly what it's like, a giant, jagged incisor. It took precision flying by the helicopter pilot to get us on and off the rock in high seas.

- -

SKERRIES, COUNTY DUBLIN

The Vikings are also responsible for the name of the Dublin seaside town of Skerries. It comes from the Danish word skere *(Gaelicised as* sceir*), which means 'low rocky island/reef', and* ey, *meaning 'island'. While Skerries itself is not an island, the presence of the term is a reference to the islands located just offshore.*

While primarily coastal raiders, the Vikings were not averse to venturing inland. How? By boat of course. We know they ventured up the Shannon and its tributaries at least as far as Longford. Scared of nobody, these lads. Many moons ago, I surveyed the course of the River Liffey with Dublin historian Pat Liddy. We took a barge all the way upstream from Grand Canal Dock to Islandbridge, and we travelled exactly as the Vikings would have done when they ventured inland. Having been at sea for weeks, I expect these salty dogs were parched, as they cautiously paddled through the brackish waters of the lower reaches of the Liffey, or 'Liphe', as it was known at that point, taking its name from the plain through which it made its way to the sea. Earlier, it had been known as 'An Ruirthech', meaning 'strong runner' or 'fast-flowing one'. Anyway, back to 795 AD and the first recorded landing by Vikings in Dublin Bay. I can just visualise these Scandinavian rovers of the sea sniffing the air for the sweet scent of fresh water as they approached the place where Christchurch now stands. This is the confluence where the River Poddle empties into the Liffey the clean rainwater it has drained from the nearby Dublin Mountains. The Vikings know a good spot to put a longphort when they see it, and this site was just perfect. Fish, fowl and fresh water.

To this day, the River Poddle flows through Dublin, although much of its course is now underground. On my television series *Creedon's Cities*, I walked along its entire route under Dame Street, beneath the Gaiety Theatre and Temple Bar, until it emerged through a giant sluice gate in the Quay Wall. It joins the Liffey directly across from the Four Courts.

The rivers were highways for the early Vikings, who rarely ventured too far from their longships. Like the Shannon, the Liffey too was one of their superhighways. From their base at Wood Quay, they continued up the Liffey and inland. Eventually, they set up another base in what is now the town of Leixlip. Now there's a place name to savour.

- -

LEIXLIP, COUNTY KILDARE
Leixlip – Léim an Bhradáin
Léim – Leap/jump
Bradán (Bhradáin) – Salmon
So in English we call it Leixlip – and that comes from the Old Norse lax hlaup, which translates as 'the leap of the salmon'. The Irish name, Léim an Bhradáin, is true to

that original meaning, whereas 'Leixlip',
the transliteration of the Viking name, means,
well, nothing really!

IRELAND'S VERY OWN TREASURE ISLAND

Ireland is blessed with mile upon mile of magnificent coastline, but one man's beauty is a Norseman's opportunity. A monastery, of which our coastal towns had no shortage, proved irresistible to Vikings out in search of treasure and slaves and they tended to target the larger monasteries more than the smaller ones. This is also why centres like Wicklow's Glendalough and Kerry's Sceilg Mhichíl were subjected to multiple raids.

While filming a piece for *Creedon's Shannon*, I spent a glorious day on the Shannon Estuary with Dixie Collins and the men and women of Kilrush Sailing Club. Some of the party sailed out to Scattery Island, whereas I travelled in the *currach*, my inner child pulling on the oar like a Viking, as I puffed and wheezed like a Viking's grandfather. Scattery comes from the Old Norse word *scattr*, meaning 'treasure', and of course *ey*, as we know, means 'island'. This translation reveals that Scattery Island is in fact Treasure Island! I bet it was exactly that, with its monastery full of chalices and no place to hide them on a tiny island. Perhaps that is why, to this day, Scattery boasts the highest round tower in Ireland.

The Vikings raided the island on a number of occasions. Their first landing was thought to have been in 816, while the second is said to have taken place in 835. It's difficult to imagine just how petrifying it must have been for the monks as they suddenly had their island sanctuary raided by these fearsome axe-wielding men draped in animal skins. Indeed, many monks lost their lives in these raids.

By 954, however, the raiders had settled and the Norsemen of Limerick, as they became known, were now living quite peacefully on the island alongside the monks. Sadly, this harmony wasn't for the long haul, and in 1101, the Vikings of Magnus III, King of Norway, raided the island in search of its valuable cache.

You might wonder why the Vikings didn't simply ignore this tiny island amongst all the other islands in the estuary and set their sights on a larger settlement? Well, despite it being quite small in size, the gigantic round tower acted as a beacon for raiders. After all, if there was a round tower, then it meant there was a monastic settlement with valuable relics and chalices. The perfect pit-stop for a Viking. The monks and the Norsemen are now all gone, but the round tower still stands tall as a monument to the struggle between war and peace that took place on that tiny stage in the middle of the Shannon Estuary a thousand years ago.

VIKING GRAVES

There still exists in Ireland today a number of Viking graves and even cemeteries. Viking graves can be found in Antrim, Galway and Kildare, while the largest known Viking cemetery outside of Scandinavia can be found in Kilmainham. The male Vikings were buried with headstones containing swords and shields, while female Vikings (shield-maidens) had headstones inscribed with brooches.

DNA REVELATIONS

As Dixie and myself shared our few sandwiches and flask of hot tea before we left Scattery Island to the rabbits and rooks again, I asked him about the Norsemen of Limerick who had settled here and upstream. I knew they had settled and married here and that those Limerick families had developed a great reputation as brave seafarers, so much so that even Christopher Columbus had referenced them in his writings.

Dixie explained, 'Yerra, at this stage, there's Viking blood in all of us, John. The Vikings were well integrated into Irish society within two centuries of them first arriving.'

Dixie's words about there being Viking blood in most of us re-awakened my father's old line about the Creedons having ample padding. 'The Creedons were always broad in the beam, like the Viking longships that brought us!' he'd say. So, given that my father's maternal ancestry includes many Cotters (from the Viking name Ottarr) with a River Lee and Inchigeelagh connection, I decided about four years ago to take a DNA test. Sure enough, the Viking blood is evident, as the test revealed that I'm mostly British/Irish, with a hint of Scandinavian and a touch of Iberian.

THE DUNGARVAN ARGUMENT

In my eyes, Dungarvan was a Viking town. Surprisingly, however, it has yet to be formally recognised as such. In a bid to change this, the people of Dungarvan have commenced a project to try to establish a firm link between the town and the Vikings. The aim of their endeavour is to prove that Dungarvan is indeed worthy of the official designation Viking town.

Here's my two cents. The Vikings left their mark all the way down the east coast and around the south. Dungarvan is on the route from Wexford to Waterford and on to Cork, so why wouldn't they have visited Dungarvan? The setting offered them everything a Viking needed, from a safe and easy mooring to fresh water and wild fowl aplenty. There were also monasteries within striking distance, and old Viking coins and artefacts have been found in two locations nearby.

Let's not forget the solid place-name evidence too. Dungarvan is nestling in a bay overlooked by Helvick Head, which we already established has its origins in Old Norse as 'bright bay' or 'safe bay'. Also, there is a townland beside the shallow waters just to the west of the town that provides that perfect spot to pull a longship ashore and set up a temporary camp. The name of the townland is Longfort. I rest my case.

6

THE NORMANS

'Dermot MacMurrough was a prize scut.' So claimed my primary school teacher, Mrs Cussens. 'He betrayed us all and let the English into Ireland while the Irish people were sound asleep in bed.'

We all agreed with Mrs Cussens. Anything that was worth knowing, Mrs Cussens knew. She was kind to us, and we were well drilled in readin', 'ritin', 'rithmetic and religion. She had us meticulously prepared for our First Holy Communion. Needless to say, Father Harte was impressed when he came to test us on our catechism. He worked his way around the classroom of shiny shoes and faces.

His questions were met with well-rehearsed precision.

'Who made the world?'

'God made the world, Father.'

'Who was John the Baptist?'

'He was Jesus's first cousin, Father.'

'Who betrayed Jesus in the Garden of Gethsemane?'

My hand shot up. 'It was Dermot MacMurrough, Father. A prize scut, if ever there was one, Father.'

'Good man, John,' sighed Father Harte. 'That was … close. Very close. Anyone else want to try that one?'

Well, okay, I was wrong, but at least I didn't reveal my source under questioning! Suffice to say, my source was standing at the top of the class, beside Father Harte, a mild panic attack bringing a rosy flush to her cheeks.

In the Ireland of my childhood, MacMurrough and Judas were interchangeable. Both of them were prize scuts. However, in time, I came to understand that not everything we were taught in school was true. For example, at best, John the Baptist was only a second cousin to Jesus, and poor old Judas couldn't have been all bad. He was probably being bullied by the Romans, and that's why he squealed on poor Jesus. Similarly, I've discovered that Dermot MacMurrough wasn't a prize scut either, merely 'a bit of an oul' scutín'. Y'see there's more to the Norman invasion of Ireland than meets the eye.

TOWNS FOR SURNAMES

In simple terms, the Normans were originally Viking, mainly Danish. From 790 onwards they raided French soil, until the Norman leader Rollon signed a deal with the King of France in 911. Rollon would call off the attacks in return for lands in the north of the country, thereafter to be known as the Duchy of Normandy. The deal was signed at Saint-Clair-sur-Epte, and soon after, Rollon's grandson, Richard, took on the title of Duke of Normandy. He created the family name St Clair from the town where the deal was signed. St Clair eventually became the surname Sinclair. We have numerous cases of families ascribing their names to place names, but interestingly, this is an example of a town providing a surname for a family.

The Normans settled happily in this fertile land and were soon calling it home. Well, actually, they were calling it Normandy, which was as good as home if you're a Norman. But y'see, that's the thing about looting, pillaging and marauding; if it's in the blood at all, it's very hard to shake it off. So, as soon as opportunity knocked, they were off to England on the same longboats that brought them. I've seen the Bayeux Tapestry first-hand, and there they are, with William the Conqueror, sailing into Hastings in 1066 and scattering all before them, just like their Viking ancestors. As we say in Irish, *Briseann an dúchas trí shúile an chait* ('the cat's heritage breaks out through its eyes' or, put another way, the apple never falls far from the tree).

As you might expect, it was only going to be a matter of time before they did what the Romans never managed to do. They set their sights on Ireland! So why was MacMurrough considered a scut? And how did Norman words end up in our place names?

Here's the gist of it. In 1167, Dermot MacMurrough, King of Leinster, was booted off his lands by the O'Rourkes of Breffni and the King of Connaught, Rory O'Connor. Amongst other things, MacMurrough was accused of kidnapping O'Rourke's wife Dearbhfhorghaill. Dermot was banished from Ireland, but travelled to France and England to try and rustle up support in an effort to reinstate his authority back home. I expect he had friends and allies in other parts of Ireland, but his nearest friends were not in Ireland at all. They were a mere few hours away in Wales. Remember, it would probably have been more difficult to bring in reinforcements over the hills from Donegal or Kerry than to ship them from across the Irish Sea.

Dermot, with the blessing of Henry II, the Anglo-Norman King of England, enlisted the help of some old friends and trading partners from Cumbria in north Wales. These Anglo-Norman noblemen, with Strongbow, the Earl of Pembroke, as their leader, struck a deal. As they had shown in Hastings exactly a century earlier, the Normans were a lean, mean fighting machine. At the time, their archers were considered the finest in the known world. They would arrive in Ireland and liberate the lands and people of MacMurrough. In return, they would receive payment and influence in Ireland. To cement the deal, Strongbow was also promised the hand of MacMurrough's daughter, Aoife.

It was a deal made in heaven. The Normans battered the occupiers out of Leinster, took the city kingdoms of Dublin, Waterford and Wexford and reinstated Dermot MacMurrough as King of Leinster, and de facto King of Ireland. The wedding of Aoife to Strongbow was a fine affair and, of course, they all lived happily ever after. If only! Y'see, when MacMurrough died, his son-in-law, Strongbow, declared himself King of Leinster and Ireland. I can picture the panic among the courtiers as they were forced to take him aside and say, 'Eh, not so quick, monsieur! You're in Ireland now, and under Brehon Law, the title falls to MacMurrough's daughter, Aoife. So Aoife is the Queen of Ireland, and you'll be well looked after as the husband of the queen!'

Of course, having come this far, Strongbow wasn't going to give up now. He wanted it all. Back in London, however, Henry II didn't like this fellow Anglo-Norman assuming such power on an island so big and so close to Britain. Cue the second wave of Normans, who this time came to clobber Strongbow, the royal wannabe.

And so began 800 years of British rule in Ireland.

When the opportunity arose in 2016, I decided to enquire about Dermot MacMurrough. I wanted to hear the case for the defence, straight from the horse's mouth, or at least, from his closest living relative. I went to meet Morgan Kavanagh, the man who now occupies Dermot MacMurrough's seat at the head of the MacMurrough/Kavanagh family. I paid him a visit at the stunningly beautiful Borris House in the dainty village of Borris, County Carlow. Morgan can trace his lineage all the way back to Dermot MacMurrough himself and was keen to speak up for his ancestor.

'Despite the plummy accent, we're actually an Irish family,' Morgan told me.

Morgan and his wife Sarah made a compelling case for their ancestor.

'I mean, what was the man to do? He had been dispossessed, banished from the country and his clan were left hungry and bereft. It was a case of recruiting the best mercenaries he could find or else let his people starve.'

'Yes, but he still let the Normans in,' I replied.

'Henry had Ireland in his sights anyway, so if it wasn't to take out his fellow Anglo-Norman, Strongbow, he would have found some other reason. The Normans were coming anyway, as they had already shown.'

Of course, Morgan *would* say that, wouldn't he? I mean, after all, he's family. However, he does speak the truth, for in 1169, the year before Strongbow's arrival, there were a number of smaller Norman invasions, and they already had a toe-hold in Wexford and Waterford. The bottom line is, they were in, they weren't going home, and the rest is history. So what about their influence on our place names? Bienvenue á Borrisoleigh!

BORRIS, COUNTY CARLOW
Borris – An Bhuiríos
Borris means 'a borough, or self-governing settlement'.

BORRISOKANE, COUNTY TIPPERARY
Borrisokane – Buiríos Uí Chéin
Buiríos – Borough/self-governing settlement
Uí Chéin – of the O'Kanes
Borrisokane therefore means 'settlement of the O'Kane family'.

BORRIS-IN-OSSORY, COUNTY LAOIS

Borris in Ossory – Buiríos Mór Osraí

Buiríos – Borough/self-governing settlement

Mór – Big

Osraí – Ossory

Borris in Ossory therefore means 'the big settlement of Ossory'.

BORRISOLEIGH, COUNTY TIPPERARY

Borrisoleigh – Buiríos Ó Luigheach

Buiríos – Borough/self-governing settlement

Ó Luigheach – of the Uí Luigheach, name of a tribe descended from Lughaidh.

Borrisoleigh therefore means 'borough or settlement of the Uí Luigheach tribe'.

As we've already seen, words are organic and keep changing, so, in a matter of five centuries, the language of the Normans had evolved from Viking dialects, to Old French dialects, to Anglo-Norman French, which was spoken by Strongbow and the Norman elite. By the time they had become 'more Irish than the Irish themselves', they were speaking a form of 'Middle Irish', and these days many Norman families like the Darcys and Butlers are sending their children to the Gaeltacht for the summer! Similarly, it wasn't long before Anglo-Norman French was slipping into the Irish language. It's where we got the term *garsún*!

▷ Garçun – *garsún* – boy

▷ Cote – *cóta* – cloak

▷ Hatte – *hata* – hat

▷ Gardin – *gairdín* – garden

▷ Bretesche – *briotás* – temporary wooden stronghold

▷ Paleis – *pailís* – pale, meaning 'boundary fence'.

That last one, *paleis*, lends itself to one of the most evocative place names on the island of Ireland, 'The Pale'. It refers to the area inside the Norman defence line that ran in a C-shape from Dundalk in County Louth to Bray in County Wicklow, taking in parts of counties Meath and Kildare. Some of the original wooden palisade can still be seen in the grounds of Clongowes Wood College near Clane. The Pale was to represent British influence in Ireland for centuries. It also gave us the widely used expression 'beyond the pale', meaning outside the bounds of civilised behaviour. A view still held, methinks, by some within the palisade!

That Norman word *paleis* is incorporated into numerous other Irish place names, such as:

▷ Pallaskenry – Pailís Chaonraí, meaning 'the palisaded castle at Kenry', County Limerick

▷ Pallasgrean – Pailís Ghréine, meaning 'the stockade of Grian', County Limerick

▷ Pallasbeg – An Phailís Bheag, meaning 'the small stockade', County Limerick

▷ Pallasboy – An Phailís Bhuí, meaning 'the yellow stockade', County Westmeath

While most of our place names are now given in English or Irish, many of them have a deep root firmly planted in the Norman invasion of Ireland. Family names, likewise, have also been influenced by the Norman invasions. With these attacks came names like Barry, Browne, Butler, D'Arcy, Dalton, De Larghey,

Dillon, Fleming, French, Hussey, Joyce, Lucey, Roche and many more, including many names with the Fitz prefix.

Many of these family names also entered the lexicon of Irish place names as Norman influence spread throughout the country. Often it's a case of listening for the sound of a French accent in a name. For example, parts of the D'Arcy family have their roots in Arcy, in Normandy. I can still detect that soft French 'r' in many Irish accents all the way from parts of Tipperary to Ardee and Drogheda. Cork is still full of Barrys and Roches. In fact, to this day, Roche's Point marks the entrance to Cork Harbour. Mind you, the jury is out with regard to its origin. I mean, is it 'Rocher', as in 'rock', or 'Roche' as in the family name? Either way, it's originally French.

Interestingly, Dingle/An Daingean is possibly the most controversial *logainm* of them all. All attempts to settle on one version or the other have ended with a split vote. I remember during a session in Tom McCarthy's bar at the top of the town I asked musician Séamus Begley for the low-down on Dingle's full name, Daingean Uí Chúis. He told me that the full moniker translates as 'fortress of the Husseys'. Séamus explained that the Husseys were Normans who came here with Strongbow and were granted lands near Dublin and in West Kerry. Dingle was the fortress for their West Kerry operation, hence the name.

With the spread of Norman influence, the prefix 'castle' also began to appear on Irish maps. So too did the suffixes 'ville', 'town' and 'ton'. Midleton in County Cork is a good example, and Battlestown in County Wexford is an even better example, because Battle, after all, is a Norman family name.

BATTLESTOWN, COUNTY WEXFORD
Battlestown – Baile Bhatail
Baile – Townland/town/home
Batail (Bhatail) – Battle

Battlestown in this case therefore means 'townland of the Battle family'.

CASTLETOWNROCHE, COUNTY CORK

I remember once driving through Castletownroche in Fermoy, County Cork, and thinking, 'This place name has it all going on!' Castle/town/Roche, three parts, and all of them Norman.

Let's break it down.

Castletownroche – Baile Chaisleáin an Róistigh

Baile – Home/townland/town

Caisleán (Caisleáin) – Castle

An Róisteach (an Róistigh) – (of Mr) Roche

Castletownroche therefore means 'townland/town at Roche Castle'.

Its original name was Dún Cruadha, founded about 2,000 years ago on the site of a previous fortress from the Iron Age. In the late 13th century, during the Norman era in Ireland, the Anglo-Norman family de la Roche built a fortress here, hence the name Castletownroche.

One of my favourite place names of all is right in the middle of the Cork–Limerick road: the town of Buttevant. Like most, I had never given it a second thought until I got bitten by the *logainm* bug! My first theory was 'butter'. Maybe an old butter road, like the one that brought my own family from Inchigeelagh into Cork, or maybe Aván, as in Avon/*abhainn*, because the beautiful River Awbeg flows by the town? But no, I couldn't make the jigsaw fit. Earliest records from the bardic tradition give its name as Cill na Mallach, until it first appears as Butheawaunt in 1259. So how and why did an entire town change name so drastically and so suddenly?

Blame the Barrys! Yes, the Anglo-Norman de Barry family, whose ancestor Odo was part of the conquest of Britain. He fought at the Battle of Hastings and was granted lands in Pembrokeshire. The family took their name from their estate around modern-day Barry Island. Methinks they must have come to Ireland with the Earl of Pembroke, Strongbow, no less. I checked, and indeed they did. William FitzOdo de Barry was rewarded with lands in south Munster for his family's part in helping Strongbow re-establish MacMurrough's kingdom of Leinster.

Members of the de Barry family went on to become Earls of Barrymore. The barony ran from the Nagle Mountains, not far from Buttevant, through lands to the north of Cork City and around to the eastern shores of Cork Harbour, to include Little Island and Fota Island. Aha! The gates of Fota House, Gardens and Wildlife Park today still bear the giant cut-stone words 'Boutez-en-Avant', the motto on the Barrymore family coat of arms. They're the very same people who owned the equally splendid estate in Buttevant. Aha! Methinks I hear the sound of a penny dropping! The town of Buttevant takes its name from the coat of arms on the Barrymore crest.

The motto, Boutez-en-Avant, French for 'strike while advancing', suggests to me perpetual motion and non-stop conquest. It perfectly describes the family's *modus operandi* from Normandy, through Hastings, to Wales, to Leinster and down to Cork. Is it any wonder the Barrys produced so many great hurlers?

BUTTEVANT/KILLNAMULLAGH, COUNTY CORK
Kilnamullagh – Cill na Mallach
Cill – Church
Mallach (may be a variant spelling of mullach,
a summit).
Thus Cill na Mallach – 'church of the summits.'

The early forms of the name Buttevant appear in the 13th century during the Norman era, such as Butheawaunt in 1259–60, whereas records of the older name Kilnamullagh still occur in the 19th century.

- -
AWBEG (RIVER), COUNTY CORK (FLOWS THROUGH BUTTEVANT)
Awbeg – An Abha Bheag
Abha – River
Beag (Bheag) – Small/little
Awbeg therefore means 'little river'.

Prior to the arrival of the Normans, the practice of slavery was rampant in Ireland, as it was all over Europe. However, the Normans are credited with the dissolution of the practice here. Not, it would appear, for any lofty principle, but because as slaves their servants were too dependent for the Normans' liking, so they set them up with a patch of land on their huge estates and told them to 'feed themselves'. This allowed their 'serfs' a little more independence, if not a huge amount of extra freedom. A visit to many Norman castles will also reveal the estate workers' original allotments. Whatever the initial intention, this practice certainly played its own part in the famine. We had big families living on bad land with just one crop to keep the workers going: potatoes. To survive, never mind thrive, would have been next to impossible.

GLADIATORS AND BON VIVEURS

Here's a fascinating fact for you. A very notable resident of Buttevant's Churchtown was the late actor and party animal Oliver Reed. He died during the making of the film *Gladiator* and is buried in Churchtown Cemetery, not too far from one of his favourite pubs. To this day, people pay their respects by pouring an alcoholic beverage on his grave! His son even once remarked that this is the very reason nothing will ever grow on it! A bon viveur, true to the French roots of the owners!

WHATS IN A NAME? IRISHTOWN

I was always curious about the name Irishtown. I'm familiar with an Irishtown in Dublin, and another in County Mayo, but I mean, isn't every town in Ireland an Irish town? So clearly this naming convention comes from a time when the native Irish were considered 'the others', but when and by whom? Firstly, I discovered that we have 29 Irishtowns in the country, and many of them date from the late 1400s, when the Anglo-Norman government in Dublin decided that the native Irish should be told to pack their bags and be forced out of the cities and towns. The Irish language and other native traditions were taking root within the city walls, and they felt these Gaelic ways needed to be removed. So anything considered particularly Irish, including people, was swiftly picked up and placed neatly outside the city walls. Separately, other Irishtowns appeared around the country in the late 19th century on foot of the efforts of the Land League. *Ach sin scéal eile!*

I can just imagine tourists standing beside 'Irishtown' signposts for photos. After all, nothing says 'I've been to Ireland' quite like a picture beside an Irishtown sign! Counties blessed with their very own Irishtown include Antrim, Offaly, Dublin, Meath, Limerick, Wexford, Louth, Wicklow, Kildare, Kilkenny, Mayo and Tipperary.

THE ORIGINAL INFLUENCERS: NORMAN INFLUENCE ON IRISH CULTURE

Bunratty Castle, Dunguaire Castle, Carrickfergus Castle … all archaeological pearls that decorate our landscape, ones we market around the world as Gaelic treasures. Except they're not! Nope! All Norman. These castles stand as monumental reminders of our history, their crenellated towers an example of Norman grandeur, their defensive motes an example of Norman ingenuity. The names of these remarkable castles adorn signposts all over Ireland – crucial markers for American tourists, who don't have castles 'back home' and flock here to absorb the energy of their Irish ancestors. You wouldn't have the heart to say they were built by lads who came originally from France.

The Norman influence extended far beyond architecture. We owe a considerable thanks to the Normans for their influence on our law, language, food and farming practices, including wool production. Even our age-old tradition of hay-making is down to the Normans. Prior to their arrival in Ireland, our cattle were kept outside all year round, come hail, rain, snow or sunshine. The Normans, however, introduced the practice of bringing their cattle into shelter during the winter months and sustaining them with the hay they had cultivated during the summer season.

The Normans have contributed so much to who we are today. From our food to our farming, our landscape to our culture and, of course, the surnames that pepper our phone book, the Normans have truly left their imprint on our country. Had they not, well, I do believe Ireland would be all the poorer for it. So the next time you see a Tourism Ireland ad for the likes of beautiful Blarney Castle, maybe offer a silent thought of thanks to the good people who gave us these architectural treasures in the first place: the Normans.

IRELAND'S NORMAN CASTLES

ASHFORD CASTLE

Where? Cong, County Mayo

What's in a name? The place name Ashford, which features quite frequently throughout the UK, usually indicates the presence of a ford near a cluster of ash trees. The Irish name, Caisleán Cheapach Corcóige, means 'castle of the beehive plot'.

ATHENRY CASTLE

Where? Athenry, County Galway

What's in a name? Athenry comes from Baile Átha an Rí, meaning 'town of the ford of the king'.

BALLYLAHAN CASTLE

Where? Strade, County Mayo (Strade is an anglicisation of the Irish An tSráid, meaning 'street'.)

What's in a name? According to the book *The Irish Landed Gentry*, the area was originally called Athleahan when the MacJordan family first built this castle. Afterwards it became 'Baile Átha Leathain', meaning 'town of the broad ford'.

BUNRATTY CASTLE

Where? Bunratty, County Clare

What's in a name? The site of Bunratty Castle was originally a Viking trading camp. This makes sense when you realise the Irish version of Bunratty is Bun Raite, meaning 'the mouth of the (River) Ratty'. As you will remember from the previous chapter, the Vikings set up their trading camps where fresh water meets the sea – longphorts.

CARLOW CASTLE

Where? Carlow Town

What's in a Name? The Irish translation of Carlow is Ceatharlach, perhaps meaning quadruple lake, which therefore suggests that Carlow Castle (Caisleán Cheatharlach) effectively means 'the castle of the quadruple lake'. However, many scholars doubt the four lakes theory and suggest that the name derives from the Old Irish word *cethir*, meaning 'four-footed beast' (cattle) and the suffix -*lach*, which simply means 'place'. So whether it's the place of the four-footed beast or of the four lakes, there's a four in there someplace!

CLONTARF CASTLE
Where? Clontarf, County Dublin
What's in a name? Clontarf comes from the Irish Cluain Tarbh, meaning 'pasture of the bulls'. Combine this with the Irish word for castle, *caisleán*, and it becomes 'Caisleán Chluain Tarbh', meaning 'castle of the pasture of the bulls'.

DUNGUAIRE CASTLE
Where? Kinvara, County Galway
What's in a name? The name Dunguaire, or Dún Guaire, to give it its Irish name, is named after King Guaire, the legendary king of Connaught. With the word *dún* meaning 'fort', the name Dunguaire therefore translates as 'fort of King Guaire'.

ENNISCORTHY CASTLE
Where? Enniscorthy, County Wexford
What's in a name? Enniscorthy comes from Inis Córthaidh, meaning 'island of the standing stones'. Thus, Enniscorthy Castle translates as Caisleán Inis Córthaidh, 'the castle on the island of the standing stones'.

HARRY AVERY'S CASTLE
Where? Newtownstewart, County Tyrone
What's in a name? This is an unusual one, in that it was named after a local chieftain, Éinrí Aimhréidh Ó Néill (anglicised as Harry

Avery). His nickname was Harry the Turbulent. Indeed, the Irish word *aimhréidh* means 'dishevelled', 'contentious' or 'troublesome'. Either way, I expect Harry was a handful.

HOWTH CASTLE
Where? Howth, County Dublin
What's in a name? The name Howth is derived from Old Norse. The Vikings mostly named coastal features and, in this case, Howth means 'head'. So, the common practice of referring to 'Howth Head' is a bit of a misnomer.

LEIXLIP CASTLE
Where? Leixlip, County Kildare
What's in a name? This is a self-explanatory one, in that it was named after the town of Leixlip, which in turn took its name from the Viking name for the salmon weir there: 'Lax hlaup'.

MALAHIDE CASTLE
Where? Malahide, County Dublin
What's in a name? Malahide Castle comes from Caisleán Mhullach Íde. As the Irish for Malahide, Mullach Íde, means 'summit of Íde', we can deduce that Caisleán Mhullach Íde means 'castle on the summit of Íde'.

NENAGH CASTLE
Where? Nenagh, County Tipperary
What's in a name? Nenagh comes from An tAonach, meaning 'the assembly, or the place of the assembly'. Caisleán an Aonaigh therefore becomes, 'castle in the place of the assembly'.

THE GREAT MOTTE
Where? Rathmore, County Kildare
What's in a name? Rathmore comes from An Ráth Mhór, meaning

'the large fort', and the Great Motte is indeed the very fort it was named after. A motte is a large flat-topped mound that was used as a watch-out and defensive position in Norman settlements. The motte referred to here was built by the Fitzgeralds as the headquarters for Fitzgerald Manor. According to a report on Excavations.ie, 'a cist or stone-lined coffin' was uncovered here. The report adds that 'this cist contained an extended adult burial, orientated with the feet to the east in the Christian tradition'.

TRIM CASTLE

Where? Trim, County Meath

What's in a name? Trim comes from Baile Átha Troim, meaning 'town of the ford of the elder tree'. Caisleán Bhaile Átha Troim therefore means 'castle in the town of the ford of the elder tree'. Trim Castle is regarded as the largest Anglo-Norman castle in Ireland.

7

CONQUEST AND CARRAIG AN AIFRINN

Family outings to Dublin were rare enough when I was a child. I remember delivering my sister Carol Ann to St Vincent's Hospital to begin her nursing training, and there was a trip to Dublin Zoo on another occasion when we all had our photographs taken with the elephant. Without much warning, the poor animal was surrounded by 14 Creedons, all jabbering away twenty to the dozen in undulating, high-pitched Cork accents. He ran bellowing back to the elephant house. It didn't really matter; we had our pictures, or 'snaps', as my parents called them.

On the journey home to Cork, we would often spot Ireland's finest racehorses being exercised on the Curragh before an ice-cream stop in the town of Kildare. Kildare was nearly as good as the zoo. There was a great sweet shop on the left. There was a Norman castle, a cathedral, a round tower and an abbey. Here, a small boy could pretend he was Robin Hood every day. Further down the street there was a signpost pointing right for Troytown. I always read it as 'Toy town'. I knew they had just opened a Legoland in Denmark, but this sounded even better. My dad, however, would point to the letter 'R' and say, 'They're not toys up there. They're Troys, a family that came in with Strongbow.'

'Great!' said I. 'Can we go up and have a look?'

'Maybe the next time. You all have school in the morning.'

Anyway, across the street from the shop was a large pub called The Silken Thomas. I assumed it was named after a famous jockey who had bought a pub. As it turns out, Silken Thomas was even more important to the people of Kildare than a champion jockey.

As my favourite history teacher, Joe Murphy, once put it, 'He had a right ol' hop off the crowd in the Pale. He tried to rid himself and all of us of English influence for once and for all.'

He did. He tried and failed. And what happened next was to change Irish place names forever.

- - - - - - - -
KILDARE
Kildare – Cill Dara
Cill – Church
Dair (Dara) – Oak
Kildare therefore means 'church of the oak'.

- -
TROYTOWN, COUNTY KILDARE
Troytown – Baile Troy
Baile – Townland/town/homestead
Troy – Troy (family/clan)
Troytown therefore means the 'townland/home of the Troys'.

Y'see, by the late 1300s, Anglo-Norman influence, which was mostly on the eastern half of the country, began to recede even further. Irish Gaelic lords were once again asserting themselves and constantly making gains. Furthermore, many of the Anglo-Normans in Ireland were embracing Gaelic ways and wives, to the point where they were now considered 'Hiberno-Normans'. The Black Death of 1348 further weakened Norman stock here, as the Grim Reaper stalked the cities and big towns of Ireland. Norman families loyal to London were mostly clustered behind solid town walls, and so were decimated, whereas Gaelic households were mostly spread throughout the countryside and escaped the worst ravages.

To add to English woes, the Earl of Fitzgerald, whose job it was to maintain control of Ireland, was fighting a losing battle here. London was too busy with its own internal struggle, the War of the Roses, to find the time to deal with the 'Irish Question'. So the tide began to turn along Ireland's east coast, and the ripples were being felt across the Irish Sea on English shores. Through the enactment of Poynings' Law in 1494, the Dublin government was put under the direct control of Westminster.

King Henry VIII, a man not known for his patience, decided he had had enough bad behaviour in his 'back garden', as he might have viewed it, and so he ordered the suppression of Ireland. However, in 1536, the aforementioned Silken Thomas launched a full-on rebellion against the Crown. That was it! That was the final straw for Henry, who declared, 'There shall be no more Irish havin' a right ol' hop off us anymore', or words to that effect!

The rebellion was put down. He upgraded Ireland to the status of kingdom, had himself declared King of Ireland and promptly set about the task of quietening the 'noisy neighbours' for once and for all. From the mid-1500s to the mid-1600s, Henry and successive English monarchs put an end to the Gaelic order, and, insofar as they could, every possible trace of it – language, customs, place names, the lot. While some might argue that the Normans were 'invited in' or even 'married in', there is little doubt that the 'New English' marched in. They set about dismantling all things Irish: law, land, limbs, language and even *logainmneacha*.

From the mid-16th century, the Crown confiscated Irish lands on a huge scale. The plantations of Ulster, Munster, Laois and Offaly would change the face of Ireland forever. To begin with, a few small family groups were invited in by landlords to settle on private estates in the far north-east of the country around counties Antrim and Down, but the first mass plantation in 1556 gave us King's County (now Offaly) and Queen's County (now Laois), named after King Philip II and Mary I. The new county town of Offaly was to be Philipstown, which has since reverted to Daingean. Tullamore has since become the county town of Offaly. Anyone guess what happened to Maryborough, named after Queen Mary I? I'll tell you. It eventually reverted to modern-day Portlaoise!

This attempt to plant Laois and Offaly had only limited success, as the neighbouring O'Moores of Laois and the O'Connors of Offaly refused to let go without a fight. They waged a sort of guerrilla war on the colonists, many of whom eventually gave up and went home. I often think about that tradition of tenacious tackling when I pass O'Moore Park Gaelic grounds in Portlaoise.

PHILIPSTOWN AND MARYBOROUGH

Philipstown and Maryborough were the first Tudor towns in Ireland. Before they were established as Tudor towns, they were known by other names. Here's the breakdown:

PHILIPSTOWN
Original name (est. c.1540s): Fort Governor. It was given this name after a new fort was constructed on the site of O'Connor's new castle.

Second name (est. 1556): Philipstown. It was named after Queen Mary's husband, King Philip.

Current name (est. 1922): Daingean (same spelling in Irish). The Irish word *daingean* means 'fortress'. It is often referred to as the 'Fortress of Offaly'.

MARYBOROUGH, COUNTY LAOIS

Original name (est. *c.*1540s): Fort Protector. It was given this name in honour of Edward Seymour, the Lord Protector of England and Duke of Somerset.

Second name (est. 1548): Maryborough. Named after Queen Mary I, who was also known as Queen Mary Tudor.

Current name (est. 1929): Portlaoise (Port Laoise). This Irish name means 'port of the tribe of Laeighis'.

THE PLANTATION OF MUNSTER

The plantation of Munster began in 1586. It was ordered by Queen Elizabeth I on foot of an uprising by the Earls of Desmond. (The name 'Desmond' comes from *Deasmhumha*, meaning 'South Munster'.) The province proved a tough nut to crack, and the Battle of Kinsale was the eventual turning point. With the Gaelic chieftains routed, wealthy English and Welsh colonists, known as 'undertakers', moved in with tenants from England to take possession of 500,000 acres of land in Limerick, Cork, Kerry and Tipperary. They were charged with carrying out the development of new towns and creating defences against any future attacks.

The reality wasn't as the Crown might have wished. It was expected that 15,000 colonists (landowners and tenants) would hold these lands, but at best, the plantation of Munster saw 3,000 or 4,000 English Protestants settle in Munster. Considerable tracts of land were simply 'sold on', and estate workers were quite often local rather than imported. For the first few years of the project, London provided small detachments of soldiers to protect individual estates, but within a few years, this support was withdrawn. The planned new towns didn't really materialise either, and planters found themselves isolated and subjected to frequent attack. Many of them returned to England or retreated to live within the existing garrison towns in Ireland.

The town of Bandon is a remarkable part of the legacy of the plantation of Munster. It was founded in 1604 by Protestant settlers for Protestants only. Catholics were to live outside the walls of the town. In the 1830s, Bandon boasted seven Orange lodges, whereas the city of Cork had only six. This monocultural society earned the town the moniker, 'Bandon, where even the pigs are Protestant'.

It's said that the following sign appeared on the gates of the town:

'Entrance to Jew, Turk or Atheist

Any man except a papist.'

To which some local wag added:

'The man who wrote this wrote it well,

For the same is writ on the gates of Hell!'

In my travels I've noted that intercultural tensions are most likely to reach snapping point where opposing views are forced to share a confined space. I witnessed this first-hand in the Middle East and in Central America, where I saw the fabulously rich living side by side with the extremely poor. The same could be said of life in South Africa today. It should be of little surprise then that some of the most bitter moments in the conquest of Munster and the eventual War of Independence were witnessed within 30 miles of Bandon. Michael Collins was born out the Clonakilty Road at Sam's Cross, and West Cork was the location of the Kilmichael Ambush and home to Tom Barry's Flying Column.

I grew up in Devonshire Street North in Cork City. There's another one across the city at Devonshire Street West. Both are named after the aristocratic landlord who owned substantial lands in Cork, and both have lasted the test of time in Cork City, whereas Devonshire Street in Bandon became Allen Street to honour the Fenian leader William Philip Allen, who was one of the Manchester Martyrs. Modern-day Connolly Street was originally Boyle Street after Lord Richard Boyle. This naming and renaming of places never ceases. The plantation of Munster, however, has left its mark on the place names of the province.

Here are just a few examples of Ireland's 'British-esque' place names:

▷ Bagenalstown, County Carlow – named after Walter Bagenal. However, this name and the original Gaelic name Muine Bheag ('small thicket') today exist side by side.

▷ Edgeworthstown, County Longford – named after Elizabethan settlers, the Edgeworth family.

▷ Randalstown, County Antrim – the Irish for Randalstown is Baile Raghnaill, which means 'Raghnal's town'. It was originally known as 'Iron Mills', but was later renamed after Randal MacDonnell, the 1st Marquess of Antrim and son of the 1st Earl of Ulster.

▷ Rockshire, County Kilkenny – This would seem to be an English name, subsequently rendered in Irish as 'Scair na Carraige', meaning a 'share of the rock', where 'shire' was perhaps mistaken for 'share'. Rockshire is very near Waterford and has been included many times in counties Waterford or Kilkenny as boundaries were revised.

IRELAND'S 'NEW'S

The prefix 'new' seems to indicate the presence of settlers. New Ross, for example, was a town built by the Anglo-Normans in the Middle

Ages. Here are just a few of Ireland's 'New's:

▷ Newtownballynoe, County Cork – The Irish version of this name is An Baile Nua, meaning 'the new town'. It's a town with its own name twice in the title. It really is called Newtown–Ballynoe. On enquiry, a native told me "Tis like New York, New York: so good we named it twice!'

▷ Newtwopothouse, County Cork – A sign I have passed on the road since I was a little boy is Newtwopothouse near Mallow. I never knew what the origins were until I enquired. It seems there were only two pot houses built in the area, and this particular one was the latest. I was thinking that maybe a pot house was a *poitín stil*. Close, but not quite. A pot house was a term used for a British tavern consisting of a bar and public rooms. There would usually be two large beer pots placed outside the pot house, almost like an early form of advertising. It appears that there was also an Oldtwopothouse, but the name was changed to Hazelwood by a landlord in the 1800s.

▷ Newtownmoneenluggagh, County Kildare – Convert the name into Irish, and you get An Móinín Logach, which means 'the pitted small bogland'.

▷ Newtownmountkennedy, County Wicklow – The Irish translation for this famous spot is Baile an Chinnéidigh, which very aptly means, 'Kennedy's town'. The updated version, Newtownmountkennedy, one of Ireland's longest place names, was founded in the mid-1600s by Sir Robert Kennedy.

▷ Newtownabbey, County Antrim – This list would not be complete without Newtownabbey. In Irish, it is Baile na Mainistreach, meaning 'the town/home of the abbey/ monastery'.

IRELAND'S LONGEST PLACE NAMES

While Newtwopothouse is the longest name in Cork, it got me thinking about the longest place names in Ireland.

Glassillaunvealnacurra (Glasoileán Bhéal na Cora), Connemara, County Galway. It means 'the green island at the mouth of the weir'. *Glasoileán* could also denote a peninsula.

Illaungraffanavrankagh, Gleninagh, the Burren, County Clare. This long place name clearly comes from the Irish. The original name was probably 'Oileán ghrafain na bhfrancach', meaning the 'the island swarming with the rats'. (Curiously, *francach* also means 'french person'!)

Muckanaghederdauhaulia (Muiceanach idir Dhá Sháile), Moycullen, County Galway. Galway certainly seems to be in a league of its own when it comes to long place names. The original Irish tells us it means 'the pig-marsh (from *muic* and *eanach*) between two sea-inlets'.

Ballywinterrourkewood (Coill Bhaile Mhuintir Ruairc), Rathkeale, County Limerick. This is a prime example of a place name originating from the presence of a local clan. In this case, the name means 'the wood of the Rourke townland'.

Corragunnagalliaghdoo Island (Carraigín na gCailleach Dubh), Burrishoole, County Mayo. The meaning behind this extraordinarily long name is a nod to the presence of the cormorant birds (*cailleacha dubha*) in the area. The

Irish means 'the little rock of the cormorants'. Mind you, *cailleacha dubha* is translated literally as 'nuns in black'.

BRITISH INFLUENCE

British influence was always going to be strongest in the larger cities and garrison towns. It's how it has always been. During the Troubles in Northern Ireland, British influence was generally greater around Belfast and staunchly loyalist towns in the north-east, whereas border areas like South Armagh and the City of Derry have been more nationalist. This ebb and flow is reflected in many of the place names, particularly along the border.

Coming in from the 'Saturday Western' at the Palace Cinema, it was hard not to make the connection between where I had just spent the afternoon and what my dad was watching on the old black-and-white Pye 18-inch in the corner. I had just seen *The Oregon Trail*. The cavalry was escorting new settlers across the Wild West. Womenfolk an' chillun' peered nervously from chuck wagons as scrawny Apache watched from behind the horizon until, fuelled by 'fire-water', the pesky injuns unleashed a light shower of arrows and rushed the wagon-train. Women screamed and injuns fell – their arrows and blood-curdling yells were no match for the guns of the well-drilled cavalry, who safely escorted the settlers back to the fort. I mostly felt sorry for the women, children and the Apache.

Back in our kitchen, I'm trying to have my tea while Charles Mitchel is reading the six o'clock news. The British Army is being rushed by scrawny natives in parka jackets, hurling rocks and insults, as the well-armed convoy makes an orderly retreat to barracks. The principle is an old one. To have and to hold. For king and country. This philosophy wasn't unique to Britain. Over the centuries, the native people of the Americas, Africa, Asia and Australia would be subjected to the same modus operandi, as the superpowers of Europe stamped their names and their footprints all over the world.

It's pretty much how it was here at the time. By 1614, the Catholic majority in the Irish parliament was eroded by a form of gerrymandering that saw new boroughs created which were then populated by English settlers. Attempts to convert the native Irish Catholics to Protestantism were brutal, fuelling a resentment so deep that in some quarters Protestantism and colonialism were viewed as indivisible. The Catholic gentry fought back and actually governed the country as 'Confederate Ireland' for a brief few years in the 1640s, before Cromwell and his armies arrived and put paid to that idea. Catholic lands were seized and given to English settlers, to have and to hold.

The native Irish were given a stark choice: 'To Hell or to Connaught'. To this day, Gaelic place names and family names are more prevalent in Connaught and on the rocky peninsulas of the west coast. In essence, Gaelic culture is richest where the land is poorest. The best lands were confiscated, monasteries were burnt and monks slaughtered, and by the time Cromwell had finished the subjugation of Ireland, half the population was dead or banished. The vulnerability of the planted families surrounded by hostile natives fanned the flames of a siege mentality. That's the problem with seeking 'the promised land'. It's just that: 'promised land'. You now have to hold it.

FIELD NAMES

One of the surest ways to denote change of ownership is to rename, and rename they certainly did. Thousands of acres of forfeited lands were subsumed into the estates of the 'New English'. Countless field names and minor names disappeared completely. Field names like

Buckley's Hollows or Tadgh O'Donnell's Meadow became Field A, Field B and so on. The original names were erased, lest any notion of ownership survive in the folk memory.

Some fields still bear the names of previous owners, who are long since on the other side of the sod. John McCullen of the Meath Fields Project told me of an occasion when a busload of Americans enquired where they might find Nicky McQuillan's Field. John pointed them in the right direction and said, 'That one is known locally as Nicky McQuillan's field but no one around here knows who he was.' In the course of the conversation, John discovered that Nicky had sold his field and emigrated to Ohio in 1837. His name, however, stayed in Ireland, and lives on in the same spot where he last pulled out the door behind him, almost two centuries ago.

At the now sparsely populated townland of Loch Con Aortha in Connemara, I met Seosamh 'Josie' Ó Súilleabháin and his two snow-white Connemara ponies. The three of them were in a small field beside the house, a green oasis in a desert of granite and limestone. 'Yerra, they're two right *peataí*!' he said as he stroked a soft muzzle. One of the mares, twitching away a horsefly, shook a long, silky mane. It glistened in the sunlight, and I could see precisely why the Atlantic waves galloping to shore with the wind whipping a spray of foam from their crests are often referred to as *capaillíní bána* ('little white horses').

Like most of his contemporaries, Josie took the boat to England and worked as a carpenter. He plied his trade on the restoration of the stylish Dorchester Hotel and had many great adventures there, including a game of snooker with Ringo Starr. But Josie eventually answered the gnawing call of home. We spoke of rural decline and depopulation. Josie fondly remembered a time when the voices of children could be heard echoing around the valley and every rock had a name. He pointed out Átha Pháidín Stiofán, a rock that functioned as a concealed poitín-maker's malt kiln. It took a lot of squinting before I finally picked it out. There's no outline to be seen when it's rock against rock, perfectly camouflaged. Further on was a fissure in the hill.

'That's Cosán an Railway,' Josie points out, referring to a shortcut the men would take when they were working on the construction of the new Galway–Clifden railway line in the 1890s. 'Over there by the lake, do you see that big stone with the tuft of grass growing at the top of it? That's Cloch a' Chaipín, the stone with the cap'. In amongst all the other boulders on the hill, it did indeed look as though one man in a crowd was wearing a cap.

Apart from deepening a community's relationship with the place, the naming of small features also has a practical side. If a sheep was lost, you had to be able to name the spot on the landscape where it was last seen. Often, in the West Cork summers of my childhood, I would leave a note for my best friend hidden under a designated stone below on the main road. We were living at opposite ends of the parish, but any time either of us was going to the village church or shop, we would know which stone to check. 'It's Thursday night for training this week. Seven o'clock. Meet you at the pitch.'

Josie told me of what can only be described as a *meitheal na logainmneacha*. In a remarkable coming together, everyone from the village, whether living at home or abroad, joined forces to walk the land and log the name, history and GPS co-ordinates of every minor *logainm* in the townland. Elderly neighbours rested on the drystone wall and pointed out the various features, their names and their stories. The flasks of tea and picnic baskets have long since been put away, *agus tá roinnt eile de na sinsir imithe ar shlí na fírinne, ach dar ndóigh, tá na logainmneacha, an dinnseanchas agus an béaloideas againn fós.* In other words, some of the elders who passed on 'the lore of place' that day have since departed for 'the way of truth', but the memory of place survives, and the website is now a living record of Loch Con Aortha.

LOCH CON AORTHA, COUNTY GALWAY
Loch Con Aortha could, quite literally, be translated
from the three key components:
Loch meaning 'lake'
Con meaning 'hound'
Aortha meaning 'shepherd'.
I'd like to think its name might be something like
'Sheepdog Lake'. There are several theories in local
folklore, but neither Josie, nor anyone I met that
weekend, would commit to a definitive meaning.

ULSTER SCOTS

If they weren't so serious, borders would be hilarious. I mean, think of it, a group of men in a room with a big table and a pen. Right, we'll draw a line through here, might as well follow the river there for a while, that's fairly obvious there. Do you think the other crowd will settle for this? Are we happy to settle for that? Right! There we go, a country! They drew a nice straight line across North America, but my experience has shown the people of Alaska have more in common with their neighbours in Canada than they do with their fellow Americans in Texas.

Similarly, the Indian spiritual teacher Anthony de Mello tells a great story about an Indian soldier captured by Pakistani troops during a border skirmish. Having been held captive for some time, the Pakistani troops march him to the top of a nearby hill and taunt, 'Here, before you die, take one last look at the hills of your beloved India. It's the last time you will set eyes on your native land.' The Indian soldier wept as he gazed upon the land for which he was willing to die. After a few moments, one of the Pakistani troops interrupted his comrades to say, 'Eh, sorry, we are actually facing the wrong way. That's still Pakistan you're looking at. India is over there, a few miles further on to the south.'

Although we are inclined to read the map of these islands from north to south, as they are politically arranged, I'm enthralled by the cultural lines that run from west to east. To my Cork ear, the accents of Donegal, Derry, Belfast and Glasgow are not a million miles removed from one another. Glasgow's old football rivalry of Celtic and Rangers is also mirrored in the green or blue football clubs of Edinburgh and Belfast. Political loyalties are predominantly arranged along similar lines.

Traditionally, migratory patterns of these islands have followed the same fault lines. Donegal tattie pickers and tunnel tigers once knew their way around Scotland like the B&I Ferry workers and Ford Motor workers of Cork once knew the streets of Swansea and Dagenham. Indeed, Cork and Welsh accents are so sing-song similar, some wag once described the Welsh as 'Corkonians who couldn't swim'. Those who could, made it to the promised land! Again, whenever I imagine a line through Dublin, Liverpool and Birmingham, I hear a musical similarity in the *canúint* (accent) of those three cities. All have proud traditions of trade unionism and music-making, and all three lay claim to the title 'Real Capital of Ireland'.

Similarly, many words have travelled across that east–west axis. This notion of mine was further compounded by a trip to beautiful Glencolumbkille. I was joined by a local guide and all-round gas man, who told me his name was Paddy Bugg. He brought me on 'An Turas', a gruelling pilgrimage from the Protestant church at the foot of the hill on a winding pattern through a series of pagan and Christian rituals.

I thought Donegal was all O'Donnells, Gallaghers, Boyces and the like; I wouldn't normally associate Bugg with Donegal.

'Is your surname spelt B - u - g - g?' I asked.

'No, I'm Paddy Bugg, B - e - a - g.'

'B - e - a - g spells *beag*, which is the Irish word for "small"?'

'Aye, that's it! Bugg. B - e - a - g!'

Not for the first time I was enthralled by the sweet rolling accent, unique to this corner of Donegal. None of the clipped tones of 'Sythe Derrie' or 'T'rone', but soft rolling r's and a tone like Dana and Daniel O'Donnell, as though butter wouldn't melt in their mouths.

'Even the way you pronounce 'Arrr-an' sounds Scottish, and nothing like the Irish- or English-speaking residents of the other Aran a few miles down the coast,' I said.

'That'll be the lowland Scots for ye,' replied Paddy.

The Plantation of Ulster was the most thorough. All the new settlers had to be English-speaking, and were drawn from the Scottish lowlands and the North of England. They brought their words with them, and to this day I hear place names in Ulster that sound totally alien to my southern ear. I once took a train from Belfast's Victoria station to Derry. The scenery seemed just like any other Irish train journey: grazing cattle and hedgerows bursting with furze and hawthorn. But the place names on the station platforms felt alien to me: Lanyon Place, Yorkgate, White Abbey, Barmouth, Umbra, Eglinton.

The place names in Northern Ireland include a colourful mix of Irish, English and Ulster Scots. Towns developed during the Plantation of Ulster include: Coleraine, Dungannon, Strabane and Ballyshannon across the border in Donegal, all from the original Irish names Cúil Raithin, Dún Geanainn, An Srath Bán and Béal Átha Seanaidh.

I have always liked the sound of the name Newtownards in County Down, and on enquiry, I discovered that it has had a varied past. In 540 AD, St Finnian founded the settlement called Magh Bhile, meaning 'plain of the sacred tree', for indeed the site was originally a pagan place of worship with a large sacred tree. In English the abbey is known as Movilla Abbey. In 1226, the Normans established a new town around Movilla and called it Nove Ville de Blathewyc, meaning 'new town of Blathewyc', based on an existing

Gaelic place name. As *bláth* is the Irish word for 'flower', there might have been a bloom or two in the area, or perhaps it was named after Saint Blathmac, an eighth-century saint and poet. Eventually Norman influence in the town went into decline, and the place became known as Ballylisnevin.

BALLYLISNEVIN, COUNTY DOWN
Ballylisnevin – Baile Lios Nevin
Baile – Town/home place
Lios Nevin – Nevin's fort
Ballylisnevin therefore means 'the town of Nevin's fort'.

In 1605, as part of the Plantation of Ulster, Viscount Hugh Montgomery of the Great Ards in Ayrshire was granted the lands. He rebuilt and christened the place Newton. He brought in Scottish settlers who elongated the name to Newton-Ards in honour of their own Scottish heritage. I give you: Newtownards!

Many words introduced by the settlers spilled over the border. The border county of Cavan is one of my favourites. Writer Michael Harding and I walked the stunning Killykeen/Coillidh Chaoin Forest Park, where the River Erne widens and pauses on its journey. We spoke about Michael's book *Staring at Lakes*, about the healing power of landscape and place. 'If you sit and listen carefully, sometimes a place will name itself.' Michael has a point. Consider a place like Gaoth Sáile (Gweesalia) in Mayo. The Irish name means 'sea breeze'. I like the sound of that.

There's a small townland called Feohanagh/An Fheothanach in West Kerry which has been given as 'faded place' or even 'place of thistles', but a colleague of mine from the area gave me an entirely different and beautifully descriptive meaning. Let's break it down. There's the word *ceo*, which means 'fog', and then there's the word *feo*, which means 'a very soft mild fog or mist'. Feohanagh therefore means 'the place that is misty', so to speak, and that's exactly what it is. Quite often, light clouds drift inland on the prevailing soft south-westerly breeze and become lodged inside there.

Another place that comes to mind is a famously windy road situated between north Clare's Ballyvaughan and Lisdoonvarna. If you have ever cycled or driven that famous road, with its arcs and curvatures, you will know it is much deserved of its now iconic nickname: Corkscrew Hill.

WHINNY HILL

Whinny Hill in County Down does not suggest that a horse lives there! Whin is the word used in Scotland for 'gorse/furze'. The word, just like the plant itself, has taken root all around Ulster and the border counties. Similarly, the word kirk, meaning 'church', has also been imported into Ulster from Scotland. Here you might be more likely to encounter a Kirkbride; south of the border it's more likely to be Kilbride (from Cill Bhríde, meaning 'Brigid's Church').

Indeed our day out in County Cavan brought us on to the Church of Ireland St Fethlimidh's Cathedral at Kilmore. Gaelic names and Protestant churches sharing the same patch of ground – I love it! I have always felt that most borders are porous, and I sense it powerfully in Cavan. As we wind our way through the rolling hills, or 'basket of eggs', as they call it, I'm reminded of England's Lake District and parts of Wales. This is drumlin country, and these elongated glacial deposits, dropped over twenty thousand years ago by the retreating ice sheet, are all lined up and pointing in the direction the glacier took. The hills roll all the way across the border into Armagh and beyond. Border? What border? It's as if the two jurisdictions overlap here and at other points along that political line on a map. I once asked a man outside Forkhill, County Armagh, how I might know if I was south or north of the border.

'Aye, the border checkpoints are gone, but whenever you see the tricolours, you'll know you're back in the North!' he laughed.

In Cavan, we met a Protestant sheep farmer speaking with a broad country accent who insisted we stop for tea and biscuits. His wife showed me a framed piece of embroidery, depicting a Norman castle with shamrock motifs in the corners.

'It's beautiful,' I acknowledged, 'but do you find it strange that Cavan is administered politically from Dublin, yet plays its Gaelic games in the Ulster Championship, and that your church diocese straddles both jurisdictions?'

''Tiz quare, right enough,' she agreed, 'but we all get along fine around here.'

We left it at that.

On another occasion, I met with Armagh man Declan Fearon at the parish church of Drumintee, 50 yards from the border, on the Dublin–Belfast road. Declan's family run a furniture business in Newry and he illustrated perfectly the folly of a hard border between Northern Ireland and the Republic of Ireland. He explained how, in the era of border patrols and custom checks in both jurisdictions, a simple furniture delivery to Dundalk could take up to three hours. These days the same trip can be done in 20 minutes. We visited the churchyard at Drumintee, where Declan's parents are buried. The church is in Northern Ireland, while the adjoining cemetery, a few feet from the wall of the church, is in the Republic of Ireland.

'I can come to Mass here,' Declan told me, 'but in the future, I may have to bring my passport if I want to put flowers on my parents' grave.'

We had parked at the nearby Carrickdale Hotel and, as we strolled back to collect our cars, he chuckled as I pointed out the irony of a name like Carrickdale. It's perfect for its position right on the border, because the name is a compound of two words: one particularly Irish word, *carraig*, and one particularly English word, 'dale'.

CARRICKDALE, COUNTY ARMAGH
Carraig – Rock
Dale, an English word meaning 'valley'.
Carrickdale therefore means 'the rocky valley'.

DRUMINTEE, COUNTY ARMAGH
Drumintee – Dromainn Tí
Droim – Ridge
Teach (an Tí) – (of the) house
Drumintee therefore means 'the ridge of the house'.

The whole border region is full of fantastic anomalies. Sometimes, it's like entering a house with a doormat across its threshold. You're never quite sure when you're in and you're never quite sure when you're out.

At St Fethlimidh's Cathedral, part of the United Dioceses of Kilmore, Elphin and Ardagh, which straddles the border, we viewed the remarkable work of Bishop William Bedell. He was responsible for the Bible being translated into the Irish language so that it could be accessible to the native population. He was severely censured by his superiors, and described by many of his community as a 'papist' and a 'Byzantine'. I concede that, yes, Bishop Bedell was partially motivated by the prospect of native Irish Catholics converting to

Anglicanism, but he did for his flock what no one else, including their own Church, had done for them. He made the Bible available to them in their own language.

I was in Derry for Fleadh Cheoil na hÉireann in 2013. Although Ulster trad musicians and fans have travelled the island in huge numbers supporting the Fleadh for years, the festival had never been staged north of the border before this. Foyleside put on a fantastic show, and Guildhall Square was packed as I found myself in front of a young man selling burgers from a van. He was all ketchup and enthusiasm.

'You're very welcome to Derry, John. A great day for the city. We've waited long enough. Here, you can have my wristband as a keepsake.'

He removed his green rubber wristband and popped it into the steaming brown bag. When I took it out of the bag, I saw the wristband read 'Tiocfaidh ár Fleadh'. I still have it.

We presented a special radio show in the neo-Gothic guildhall, with its replica Big Ben clocktower.

I looked up at an imposing figure wearing his robes of office on the stained-glass window. The inscription read 'Lord Aberfoyle'. I returned to Penny at the front desk, who had given me my 'access all areas' laminate earlier. She cracked the code for me within seconds.

'*Aber* means "the mouth of a river". It's Scots Gaelic,' she explained. This got me thinking. Aberfoyle is the area around the mouth of the River Foyle. Aha! So Aberdeen means 'mouth of the River Deen'. Then there's Abercrombie in Scotland, and you have quite a few Abers in Wales too, like Aberystwyth.

THE GUILDHALL, DERRY

Guildhall – Gildhalla, based on the historical English term; formed from *gild* (a trade guild) and *halla* (a hall).

Built in 1887, it was originally named Victoria Hall, in honour of the ruling British monarch. It was officially opened in 1890 as the administrative centre for Londonderry Corporation. The current name honours the Guildhall's connection to the City of London and its guilds. It is where the elected members of Derry and Strabane District Council currently meet and is also home to the Derry City Council chamber and the Mayor's Parlour. Events from craft fairs to weddings are often held here.

This is the most significant one in Ireland. In Dublin, guildhalls tended to be named after the guild in question, e.g. Weavers' Hall, Bricklayers' Hall, Merchants' Hall, Tailors' Hall.

On another occasion, while making *Creedon's Atlas of Ireland*, our producer, Mary Martin, arranged a meeting with Dr Frances Kane from the Queen's University Place Names Project. We walked the walls of Derry, where I asked her to give me the definitive name for the city. Is it Derry or Londonderry?

'To be fairly honest, neither!' Frances laughed. 'The element "Derry" is actually pretty common in place names, in that it's an anglicisation of the word *doire*, meaning "an oak wood" or "an oak grove". In the 1600s, English settlers started to arrive, and many were unable to pronounce "Doire" so it was pronounced and eventually spelled "Derry".'

Frances went on to explain that where the city now stands was once an island. A channel of the River Foyle flowed through part of the island, but whenever the channel dried up, it left boggy land in its wake, so the locals called it what it was, and Derry's famous Bogside was christened. Elementary, really. Given that the Irish word for 'soft' is *bog*, I sometimes wonder if the word bog, meaning a soft marshy area, originated here in Ireland?

The Bogside is home not only to some of the world's most iconic murals, but also to the punk rock band The Undertones. After speaking with Dr Kane that evening, I headed down to the Bogside Inn to catch up over a beer with Undertones singer Paul McLoone and bass player Mickey Bradley. While Paul had grown up in the Bogside, Mickey was from nearby Creggan (An Creagán, meaning 'a stony place'). When I pressed the lads for the definitive version of the city's name, Mickey cited a most unusual source, given the neighbourhood in which we were sitting. He quoted the unionist politician Glenn Barr, who once replied to the same question with absolute clarity: 'I don't mind what you call it, as long as you don't mind what I call it!'

The Bull Park was a name the lads often referenced, and it was one that interested me greatly. I asked them what it was.

'To us, it was a playground. That's where you played football and sort of, well, sat on a wall!' Mickey replied. 'Then when it came to the time we were making our first LP, the local photographer Larry Doherty, who worked for the *Derry Journal*, was going to take the photographs, so the obvious place for us to gather was in the Bull Park. That photo became the cover of the album!'

I asked the lads if they knew why it had been given the name the Bull Park. Mickey surmised it must have an association with the slaughterhouse 'down the road'. Indeed, he was bang on. According to the Ordnance Survey mapping carried out by Major General Thomas Colby, who documented Derry to a considerable degree, the Bull Park was once a cattle market. So, in its lifetime, it was a bull park a ballpark, and the cover of a famous album! Whatever would Colby think?

TRANSLATING BUNOWEN

Some Ulster Scots words have leaked over the border. County Donegal's Burnfoot, for example, comes from the word *burn*, meaning 'stream'. Burnfoot therefore means 'the end of the stream'. This could be translated into Irish as Bun na hAbhann, which could then be anglicised as Bunowen. I feel we may have inadvertently stumbled across the place name that gave Brian Friel the inspiration for the mythical town of Bunowen, which was at the centre of his play *Translations*. I wonder if the idea crossed his mind as he passed the nearby sign for Burnfoot?

CARRIGANAFFRIN

'For every action, there is an equal and opposite reaction.'

So states Newton's Third Law of Motion. It's a golden rule of physics. It always struck me as a rule that can also be applied to the physics of conquest. You can push people all the way to the wall. But eventually you'll get an opposite reaction and they'll push back.

The intention of the Plantation of Ireland and of the subsequent Penal Laws (1691–1760) was to crush any opposition to outright English rule in Ireland. Land was confiscated and renamed. The Irish language was outlawed and so too were Catholicism and Protestant dissidents. Priests were hunted down, tortured and killed.

However, for all of their efforts, the language and religion of the native Irish was never quite dead and buried. It was merely pushed underground, but never the full 'six feet under'. Catholic schools were closed, but little 'hedge schools' gave a rudimentary education to the poor. Children were versed in English, Irish, mathematics, Gaelic culture and, in some cases, even Latin. Gaelic culture was clinging on by its fingernails. The memory of these hedge schools is preserved in *logainmneacha* like Scoil Chois Claí ('school by a ditch/ fence'), Scoil Ghairid ('temporary school') and Scoil Scairte ('school of the hedge').

Priests were on the run, and Irish Catholics would risk the point of a sword by harbouring them. Mass was celebrated in remote locations, quite often at night, with little more than a slab of rock serving as a crude altar. Sometimes the priest was veiled from the congregation, lest he be identified. These Mass sites still feature in *logainmneacha* and minor place names all over Ireland.

- - - - - - - - - - - - - - - -
CLAIS AN AIFRINN
Clais – trench, ravine
Aifreann (an Aifrinn) – (of the) Mass
Clais an Aifrinn therefore means 'the Mass trench'.

- - - - - - - - - - - - - - - -
PÁIRC AN TSÉIPÉIL
Páirc – Field
Séipéal (an tSéipéil) – Chapel
Páirc an tSéipéil therefore means 'the chapel field'.

- - - - - - - - - - - - - - - -
GLEANN AN AIFRINN
Gleann – Glen
Aifreann (an Aifrinn) – (of the) Mass
Gleann an Aifrinn therefore means 'the glen of the Mass'.

LEACA NA HALTÓRACH

Leac – Slab

Altóir (na hAltórach) – (of the) Altar

Leaca na hAltórach therefore means 'the altar slab'.

CNOC NA HALTÓRACH

Cnoc – Hill

Altóir (na hAltórach) – Altar

Cnoc na hAltórach therefore means 'the hill of the altar'.

Many rural communities still gather at local Mass rocks and holy sites. After a gap of more than four centuries, Canon Island, where the River Fergus meets the Shannon Estuary, has again begun to host an annual Mass. An Augustinian abbey was established there in 1189, and it housed a community of Canons (a form of secular clergy). The abbey thrived until Henry VIII ordered the dissolution of the monasteries. When Cromwellian forces bombarded the island in 1651, the abbey was finally decimated, and the church fell silent.

CANON ISLAND, KILLADYSERT, COUNTY CLARE

Canon Island – Oileán na gCanánach

Oileán – Island

Canónach/Canánach (na gCanánach) – of the canons

In the 1970s, the last of the families who inhabited the archipelago of islands in this part of the estuary came ashore. Many of them now live in the nearby County Clare village of Killadysert (Cill an Dísirt, meaning 'church of the wilderness'). I attended the Mass at Canon

Island a few years ago. Fergal Ginnane and his father Fintan took me and two or three others to the island in a small boat. Another man in his 40s wearing a windbreaker was seated beside me. He introduced himself as Fintan Monahan.

'Another Fintan?' I queried. 'Ah! You must be an islander so?'

'No, I'm actually from Tullamore, County Offaly, originally, but I'm the Bishop of Killaloe for my sins now,' came the reply!

Over the whine of the outboard motor, Fergal pointed out various islands:

- ▷ Inishcorker – Inis Carcair, meaning 'island of the prison' – or it could possibly mean 'island of the large rock/stump'.

- ▷ Coney Island – Oileán na gCoiníní, meaning 'island of the rabbits'. This place name is found all over, from Ulster to New York!

- ▷ Inishtubbrid – Inis Tiobrad, meaning 'island with a well'.

- ▷ Inisherk – Inis Eirc, meaning 'Erck's island'. A viking, I expect.

- ▷ Low Island – Inis Luanus, meaning 'the island of St Luanus'.

- ▷ Horse Island – Inis Mhic Uaithne, which has resulted in the island often being referred to as Inishmacowney. This is where the Ginnane family once lived, and where they still keep a few cows.

A flotilla of little boats whizz between the islands, as some of the older islanders, those who came ashore in the 1970s, revisit the now abandoned home places and recall the sound of children playing. Soon the boats are silenced and the sound of a bell and a community at prayer can be heard on the estuary again. It's difficult to stand here without feeling the presence of those who went before. Heads bowed, the men and women in front of me are led by their bishop, in a hushed call and response,

'*A Dhia déan trócaire*/God have mercy'

'*A Chríost déan trócaire*/Christ have mercy'

The rhythmic prayer carries across the water and carries me with it, back to my own *áit dúchais*.

I can visualise my own people at Carraig an Aifrinn in Inchigeelagh: women, their heads covered with shawls and men, caps removed, kneeling on the wet ground, beseeching the almighty to deliver them from the terror being meted out to them. Young volunteers on higher ground nervously watching and listening for the sound of redcoats. A momentary lapse on their part could seal a fate worse than death for their priest. Below them on the rock, he raises the crucifix.

The sound of a stifled cough returns me to Canon Island. The spell lifts as the congregation slowly returns from the world of the sacred to the secular. The murmur of self-conscious conversation is fractured by the stray voice of a child, and then the hearty chuckle of two farmers getting a story from someone else at the back.

I stay behind until the island is empty apart from the two Fintans, the bishop and the boatman. Young Fergal and an elderly man have gathered up the vessels and are carrying the crate back towards the boat. For a few moments I have the roofless abbey to myself. I eventually stretch and rise to go, placing my hand for support on the very same altar slab that an elderly priest might have placed his five hundred years ago.

Catholic emancipation and independence were eventually won, and are now taken as a given. When visiting Ireland in September 1979, Pope John Paul II recalled how the Mass has endured here through the centuries. He spoke of 'the Eucharist being celebrated at Mass rocks in the glens and forests by hunted priests'. The memory of that terrible time is fading, as is religion itself. But I can clearly remember a time when we still prayed for the canonisation of Blessed Oliver Plunkett, who was hung drawn and quartered in 1681. I remember overflowing churches where the soaring crescendo of

'Faith of Our Fathers' would reverberate from the highest rafters in wave after wave of defiance.

> *'Faith of our fathers! Living still,*
> *In spite of dungeon, fire and sword.*
> *Oh, how hearts beat high with joy*
> *Whene'er we hear that glorious word.*
> *Faith of our fathers! Holy faith!*
> *We will be true to thee 'til death.'*

As hymns go, this was a battle cry, but it was a cry, nonetheless.

8

FROM DOWN TO O'DONOVAN

When Ptolemy mapped Ireland in *c.*140 AD, I expect he was motivated by a sense of curiosity and a spirit of adventure. When the island was again surveyed some 1,500 years later, however, the study was driven, not by a thirst for knowledge, but by a thirst for land. The driving force behind the survey of the 1600s was none other than the infamous Oliver Cromwell.

THE DOWN SURVEY OF THE 1600S

By the time this survey began in 1656, approximately 2.5 million acres of land had been forfeited by Irish Catholics to what was now euphemistically described as 'the Commonwealth'. If anything, wealth was becoming less common. These confiscated lands were then either sold to English settlers or used by Cromwell as a means of payment to the men in his army who had carried out the conquest of Ireland. In order to map the lands that had been forfeited, and most importantly, to ascertain their value, a survey was ordered. This became known as the Down Survey. No, it wasn't the cartographer's name, nor had it anything to do with County

Down. It was so named because measurements were taken from the chains that were literally put 'down' on the ground to mark out distances.

The survey took two years to complete and was overseen by the surgeon-general of the British Army, Sir William Petty. Interestingly, Petty was himself paid with forfeited land for his survey work. He received nearly 4,000 acres in Kenmare, County Kerry. He later added another 2,000 acres of land which he had purchased from soldiers who wanted out and were moving back to Britain. We've seen similar patterns on previous occasions. Free land seems like a great idea, until you're expected to live on it and hold it 'for king and country'. Over and over again, English settlers upped sticks and took the boat back to Blighty.

Mind you, Petty himself was made of sterner stuff, and he stayed the course. Indeed, within a decade, Petty had laid out plans for the modern town of Kenmare (Ceann Mara, meaning 'headland of the sea'). The three main streets that form the triangle in the centre of the town were named William Street (which is now Main Street), Henry Street and Shelbourne Street, because William Petty's son Henry became the first Earl of Shelburne. His name was also later applied to Shelbourne Road in Dublin.

ARTICHOKE ROAD

Prior to Shelbourne Road being named in honour of Earl Henry Petty, it was known as Artichoke Road, and also Great Britain Quay. Artichoke? There's posh!

At times, I'm surprised at the level of town planning that has gone into some of our most westerly towns. Every now and then I'll find myself tootling through a landscape of bog and bulrush that suddenly gives way to a beautiful estate house, set amidst rolling lawns, with the ordered streets of the adjoining village giving an air of old England right in the heart of old Ireland. The beautiful Mayo town of Westport (Cathair na Mart, meaning 'the city of the beefs/ fatted cows' – a reference to the town's fair) is a wonderful example with its orderly streets and squares. Indeed, one of the 'squares' is actually eight-sided, and is correctly referred to as 'the Octagon'. The centrepiece of the Octagon used to feature a statue of Queen Victoria on a tall column. These days St Patrick occupies that perch.

Not unlike the pattern of towns growing up around the walls of the monasteries a millennium earlier, towns now sprouted wherever the foundations of a big house were laid. The practice continued for as long as estates needed estate workers, churches, shops and other infrastructure. We have several place names with the term 'Newtown' in the title, one of my favourites being Newtownballynoe, County Cork, which I mentioned in the previous chapter.

Knightstown on Kerry's Valentia Island is another favourite. In Irish, it becomes Baile an Ridire, meaning 'town of the knight'. The name of the village is quite an enigma, as indeed is the name of the island itself. Given the proliferation of Gaelic names along our western seaboard, I always felt the name 'Knightstown' stuck out like a bluffer at the round table. I mean, even the bravest of knights would be slow to venture this far west, right? Not so! On enquiry, I discovered that the village is indeed named after a real knight. He was Maurice FitzGerald, the 18th Knight of Kerry. In 1831 or thereabouts, he commissioned Scottish engineer Alexander Nimmo to draw up plans for a new village on the island that he had bought two decades earlier. He certainly picked a beautiful site. Situated on the more sheltered east-facing side of Valentia Island, the village overlooks a sheltered bay, speckled with smaller islands. During the 1840s, development began on what was initially known as the New Town of Valentia, ultimately becoming better known as Knightstown, after the man who commissioned it.

As for the name of the island itself? A corruption of Valencia in Spain, perhaps? I mean, given the centuries of traffic up and down the Atlantic shipping lanes between Ireland and Iberia, it would seem a reasonable hypothesis. However, the name Valentia is actually a fairly decent attempt at pronouncing its Irish name, which also describes the place perfectly. In Irish, Valentia becomes Cuan Bhéal Inse meaning, 'harbour at the mouth of the inlet'. In 1370 it was recorded as 'Tar Caladh nDairbhre', meaning 'pier of the oaks'.

- - - - - - - - - - - - - -

COUNTY KERRY

Kerry – Ciarraí (originally known as Ciarraighe)
Ciarraí/Ciarraighe – People of Ciar. Ciar was the
name of the ancestor or progenitor of a tribe that
lived in the county.

The completed Down Survey consisted of four maps: a blank overview map of the country, a map of the counties, a map of the baronies, of which Ireland had 252, and a map of the parishes, of which there were 2,278, according to the Trinity College Down Survey website. When it came to valuations, £200 in old money could buy you a thousand acres of land in Connaught, but if you wanted to buy the same acreage in Leinster, you could be looking at a bill of £600 or more.

When Cromwell condemned the native Irish 'to hell or to Connaught', the beauty of the Wild Atlantic Way wasn't quite what he had in mind. Large numbers of Irish Catholics made the sad trek west, leaving fine green pastures in the midlands and east as bounty to the English officers and soldiers who had terrorised them.

UP IN SMOKE

Did you ever press 'delete' by mistake? Do you recognise that heart-stopping feeling when shock and disbelief hits you at the very same moment? It happened to me years back when a tiny hand once reached up and pressed a key on my keyboard and deleted my entire collection of wild-bird photographs. Twenty years of work ... gone! Winded, I paced the room desperately trying to rewind my life. 'Just two minutes, God. Please! Let them be there. I'll double-check again and press "save", and I'll put away the camera forever and give the children more of my time.'

God, it would appear, was away on business that day.

That same hollow sense of loss gnaws at me whenever I hear of historical artefacts being lost forever. It's the feeling I got when the Taliban destroyed the ancient carvings of Buddha at Bamiyan, or when I watched Notre Dame burn in Paris. You can restore, but you will never retrieve. It's worse again when there is no record of what was lost. When there are no plans, no copies, no photographs. It's as if the only family photograph of your great-grandparents has been lost in a fire. And that's exactly what happened, on a national scale, with the Down Survey documents. Not once, but twice!

In the early 1700s, four entire volumes of survey material were destroyed in a fire. The records for Kerry, Clare, Galway and Roscommon – all burned to a cinder. Overall, volumes for just 10 counties remained, the survivors being Dublin, Wicklow, Wexford, Waterford, Carlow, Leitrim, Westmeath, Donegal, Tyrone and Derry. These original Down maps that survived the fire were later lost in the Custom House fire of 1922. These two events cost the entire nation our 'one moment in time' snapshot of Ireland in the 1600s.

William Petty was an academic powerhouse and considered a genius by his peers. Apart from being an accomplished mathematician, economist and statistician, he was also a physician, a professor of anatomy at Oxford, a professor of music in London and, if that wasn't enough, he was also a member of Parliament. Whatever his personal motives, it would have been wonderful for Ireland to have had Petty's original works on display today. Alas, fate and the often-all-too-cruel hand it plays had other ideas for them.

While the Down Survey certainly shed some light on life in Ireland at that time, there was still no real clear overview of the country, no insight into the lives of the people or their places. At least not until the big survey of the 1820s, the Ordnance Survey of Ireland.

A RECORD OF THINGS

The term 'Ordnance Survey' sounds so technical, but don't let this put you off. The word 'ordnance' originally referred to military weaponry. The term widened to include civilian items and now simply means 'things'. The word 'survey' means 'record', so these days an ordnance survey essentially means 'a record of things'.

THE BIG ONE – THE ORDNANCE SURVEY OF THE 1820S

By the time the 1800s rolled around, there was still no definitive map of Ireland. What we had, you could say, was a jigsaw of maps, with very little consistency. Some maps contradicted the detail in others, and measurements were often dubious. It has kept solicitors and real estate agents busy at their work for generations!

So, to begin, we had Ptolemy's map. Then came the Down Survey, followed by a colourful blend of smaller studies such as the Strafford

Survey, bog surveys, legal maps and so on. While all of these were hugely useful in their own right, there was most definitely a need for one complete map, one clear, accurate snapshot of the country. Dissatisfaction with the land taxation system finally brought the matter to a head in 1824.

To this day, enthusiasm for property tax is usually only found amongst those who don't have any property! It was ever thus. So, in 17th-century Ireland, it was common practice for farmers and landowners to declare only a fraction of their acreage in a bid to reduce their tax bill. After all, there was no valid evidence to prove them wrong.

Major General Thomas Colby, the man ultimately responsible for the mathematics of the mapping process, even went so far as to remark that Ireland was 'a mosaic of civil and military maps at various scales and accuracy'. In simple terms, it was impossible to get a handle on any farm or its size. There was only one thing for it. The country would have to be mapped again, and this time in considerable detail. The British government set up the Spring Rice Committee, whose job it was to sort out the situation.

Major Colby proposed a colossal survey of Ireland that would see it being mapped on a scale of six inches to the mile. Such a map would finally give them the specifics they needed. It was decided that the task of mapping and collating the information would be the responsibility of the Ordnance Survey Department of the British Army.

Only an empire could afford to document and map a country in such great detail and the British Empire certainly had the resources and the motivation. They had a civil service that was second to none at logging detail. The British military records and national archives are still the envy of the world. When they came to map Ireland, they mapped us well. It's generally accepted that when Colby was finished with his work, Ireland was probably the best mapped country on earth.

SURVEYING: THE ABILITY TO MAP AND WRESTLE FARMERS

Once the Boundary Survey of Ireland Act was passed in 1825, it meant the road was clear for the work to commence. It was decided to concentrate the survey on the townland boundaries, as it was felt that they would be the most suitable denominations upon which to base the tax. Before they could start, however, the boundary surveyors needed a ground basis from which to work; they needed to know where they were going, so they were each given sketch maps from a variety of earlier maps in the records office. Armed with these, the surveyors went off walking the length and breadth of the country, measuring the boundaries of every townland in Ireland.

To put it bluntly, surveying the townlands was a tough and, at times, downright horrible job. The surveyors were rarely welcomed by landowner or tenant. In fact, such was the level of animosity towards them that a newspaper advertisement offering positions as boundary surveyors detailed that candidates 'must be able to wrestle farmers'. As ridiculous as this might appear to us, I remind you of scuffles during protests against the proposed 'water tax' of 2014. Despite local resistance, the team managed to log every town, village and crossroads. Marshy bogland was marked down as such, as was forest. Ancient monuments and holy wells were all included.

While the main purpose of the survey was to establish the rateable valuation of land, the extensive mapping also served military needs. In the event of any civil unrest, a clear map of every highway, by-way and back-road would remove any 'home advantage' to the rebels, even in the most remote townland. The results of all this work, however, were a long time coming. The survey began in 1825, with Colby quoting £300,000 for the mapping process and estimating a timeline of seven years to completion. Two years into the project, there were 39 officers, 98 civil assistants, 234 people in other ranks and 303 labourers working on the survey. By 1832, more than two thousand people were employed to work on it. You can imagine the sense of frustration when the £300,000 budget ran out, and a finished map had yet to be produced.

Two decades from the date of commencement, and at a final cost of £890,000, the mapping of Ireland was finally complete. The overall findings established that the country had over 62,000 townlands varying in size from just one acre to 7,000 acres. As if life wasn't already hard enough, the days of claiming you owned only two acres, when in fact you owned 20, were well and truly over. I sometimes wonder if the survey gave rise to the practice of understating one's wealth – *an béal bocht*, meaning 'the poor mouth'?

As the survey had gone over budget by nearly £600,000, the Ordnance Survey branch was under pressure to make some of the money back, so they produced coloured versions of the map for sale to the public. Many of these were framed and displayed proudly over the fireplaces of pubs and big farmhouses. Quite a few of them still survive. Of course, Ordnance Survey Ireland, OSI, has since reproduced hundreds of thousands of maps for generations of Geography students. I had a particular *grá* for these maps, as they afforded me an opportunity to daydream in the middle of class. I would survey the landscape represented on the map and seek out a bend on the road. I'd then look for the contours denoting high ground above the road. I could spot an ambush site from six inches to the mile. Boys will be boys.

While this Boundary Survey of Ireland would have come as a source of major disappointment and higher taxes for many, the long-term value of the work far outweighs its cost to public and private pockets. Two hundred years later, engineers and surveyors still roll out the maps, so to speak, as they plan another motorway or development online. Likewise, archaeologists still refer to these maps which document the location of *fulachtaí fia*, burial chambers and other ancient monuments that dot the Irish countryside.

The actor and raconteur Niall Tóibín once described Ireland as 'an island, three hundred miles long and one hundred and fifty miles … thick!' At six inches to the mile, that's a lot of map. Visualise it if you can. Six inches of map was required to represent just one mile. So a country of Ireland's dimensions would require a single map that was 150 feet (46 metres) long and 75 feet (23 metres) wide. Colby produced 1,900 large maps to cover the entire island, a remarkable feat of mapping. Even England didn't have a map to that scale.

The work itself was painstaking and tedious. I know this first-hand! Hubert Davey and his team from Ordnance Survey Ireland invited me to join them as we mapped a small townland outside Mullingar. We did it the old-fashioned way, dragging chains across fields and through nettles, in the rain. If it weren't for the good humour of the crew and Barry Donnellan's flasks of coffee, I would have mutinied. My job was to take the front end of a rusty chain and walk ahead of the back-marker until the chain was fully extended. At that point Hubert would shout 'mark!' as only a military man can. I would insert a drop-pin into the sod at my feet to mark the spot and then walk on. When Hubert got to my pin he would shout 'Mark!' again. I'd drop the next pin, Hubert would collect the previous pin, and on we went. When we regrouped at the boundary fence or ditch, all we had to do was count all the drop-pins collected by Hubert and we had the chain measure covered. Chains, roods and perches, that's how we measured land in school.

I note that the shape of the 19th-century drop-pin has been adopted as the symbol for a drop-pin on the modern-day Google Maps. The greatest lesson I learned from my day with the OSI was this: stop whinging about the accent of the voice on my GPS, pronouncing Chapelizod as 'Chapple Lizodd' and *timpeallán* ('roundabout') as 'Tim Pellan'. Trust me, it's a minor irritation in comparison to squelching across bogs with chains to the shouts of 'Mark!'

IRELAND IN THE LIMELIGHT

The 1820s were a time of incredible innovation and invention, and the Ordnance Survey of Ireland was responsible for two fine contributions to the Industrial Revolution. Major General Colby's 'compensation bar' was one. This metal bar was designed for use when measuring base lines. Originally, chains were used to take such measurements, but the length of these chains would change if the temperature caused them to expand or contract. Colby's Bar, a brass and iron bar, joined at the centre, provided the consistency required to ensure the accuracy of such measurements. Colby's invention still stands the test of time, as I discovered in that wet field outside Mullingar in June 2019.

Lieutenant Thomas Drummond, an engineer who worked as a surveyor with the Ordnance Survey of Ireland, is credited, alongside English chemist Goldsworthy Gurney, with having developed the limelight. In essence, this involved burning a block of lime in a hydrogen-oxygen flame, producing a strong luminescent light, allowing surveyors to continue working during the hours of darkness. In the years that followed, British theatre adapted this limelight to illuminate the players on stage, hence the expression 'in the limelight'. I can almost hear the silent 'tutting' of the ghosts of British Army surveyors who spent long nights up to their knees in mud trying to crack a match.

LIEUTENANT LARCOM'S HEADACHE

The place-name collection, one of the brightest jewels in the treasure chest of information presented at the end of the survey, only came about as an afterthought. The survey was well underway, and Thomas Aiskew Larcom was the man in charge of heading up the data processing back at the headquarters in the Phoenix Park. As fate would have it, Larcom, an Englishman, had developed an interest in Irish culture. It was an interest matched only by his enthusiasm for accuracy. Let me explain. The (still) contentious Dingle versus An Daingean debate was already raging in Larcom's office in the 1820s, but it was Larcom's responsibility to sign off on the final names on the map. As the boundary surveyors were relaying the information back to the Ordnance Survey office in the Phoenix Park, Larcom began to notice a number of inconsistencies, not so much with the measurements but with the place names and their spellings. He might, for example, receive a report citing a certain number of streets in a County Kerry town spelled 'Dingle'. Another member of the team, however, might then submit a report about the number of shops in the same town, but spell it 'Dingel'. A third report might reference the town by its Irish name, 'An Daingean', while a fourth report might use its full Irish name, 'Daingean Uí Chúis'. These inconsistencies were a source of constant irritation to Larcom, surpassed only by the itch of wet tweed and midge bites to his surveyors in the field.

Larcom quickly realised there was a great need for a place-names branch within this grand survey. Every place in Ireland had at least two names – the Irish and English version – and sometimes an older name was still in use, and then, of course, there were variations in spelling. Fortunately, Larcom had the good sense to know that these names needed to be documented for posterity. More importantly, he had the courage to ask for a budget, even at this late stage in the work, to establish a topographical branch of the Ordnance Survey.

This new office was dedicated solely to gathering every place name in the country. The plan was to send out linguists, fluent in both Irish and English, to gather first-hand information about the names. Apart from researching old manuscripts, a crucial part of the task would be to verify spellings and pronunciations with locals, and not just the local clergyman or schoolteacher either. Small farmers and their wives would also be quizzed. Thankfully, Larcom was also curious about the meaning behind Ireland's place names, so he decided to include this as part of the survey. The team then would have to interpret what the names meant and why a place had been given a particular name.

The mapping process was already well under way, so the fledgling place-names office needed to get the ball rolling if they were to create this in-depth 3D record of *logainmneacha na hÉireann*. Larcom commissioned a man called Edward O'Reilly to spearhead the project. Unfortunately, the poor chap was only in the job six months when he died in 1829. It's thought that the arduous work combined with the terrible conditions hastened his sudden demise. In fairness, it was a very tough gig. Not only did the place-name surveyors have to walk the length and breadth of the country in cold, damp conditions, but life in the Irish countryside was unimaginably difficult. Remember, this was taking place in the years leading up to the Famine, the greatest single calamity visited upon the country. Those on the survey's frontline witnessed great suffering. Large families on small farms with little to their name had no appetite for such studies. It's easy to imagine a drawn and weather-beaten face saying, 'The *logainmneacha* around here are beautiful alright, but you can't ate 'em.'

After the sudden passing of Edward O'Reilly, Larcom offered the job to a Kilkenny-born academic named John O'Donovan.

Larcom had developed a great interest in the Irish language, and had in fact been taking Irish lessons from O'Donovan. It was a match made in a place name called Neamh (the *logainm* for Heaven). Both men were fuelled with a passion to explore the deepest roots of Ireland's ancient *logainmneacha*.

JOHN O'DONOVAN'S PLACE NAMES

It's interesting that Larcom's curiosity about Irish place names preceded his full understanding of the language. I feel this is significant. Quite often, our understanding of a language can get in the way of the simple joy of savouring the sound of a place name. Australian aboriginal place names such as Geelong, Wagga Wagga and Wollongong, for example, all dance for the ear. Long before I learned to speak Irish, I loved the sound of places like Keamkurrabooley as pronounced by my teacher, Mr Buckley. It sounded to me like a beach in Hawaii. It still does. The sound of the Irish word *póg* is another beauty. Not the sharp hiss of the English word 'kiss' or the Spanish *besos*, but the soft sound that requires one to actually blow a kiss when in the process of saying it. Try it!

I often wonder about the significance of the sound of O'Donovan's own homeplace in his love of *logainmneacha*. He grew up in a townland called Atateemore. Like the rat-a-tat-tat of a drum, there's an elite syncopation to the sound of At-A-Tee-More. I could well imagine the young John O'Donovan reciting it to himself as he walked the roads around Slieverue, beautiful Lough Cullen and the neighbouring parish of Scartnamoe. This land is rich in the poetry of place names. 'Atateemore ... Scartnamoe ... Atateemore ... Scartnamoe.'

From my first encounter with the work of this polymath, I was keen to see the place that formed him. Given his home address, 'place of the big house', and his academic achievements, would I uncover the son of a wealthy farmer?

I was to find out when I eventually made the pilgrimage to his birthplace in County Kilkenny. I couldn't have asked for better company. I met two men with a deep understanding of our *logainmneacha*, Dr Pádraig Ó Cearbhaill, the Chief Place Names Officer for Ireland, and retired Slieverue school principal, Jim Walsh, an authority on the life of O'Donovan. The two men led me along a country road with Waterford on view away across the fields to the south-west. Like a scene from *Last of the Summer Wine*, we ambled, engrossed in our chosen subject, down a small hill past what remains of the big house that gives the townland its name. The O'Donovan family lived in a little cottage in a hollow below the big house. I was taken aback to view the original home in ruins, little more than a gable end still standing, like a memorial stone to the family that once lit the fireplace at its base.

'This little house-ín got flooded so badly and so often that the family had to abandon ship and build this one here on slightly higher ground,' Jim explained as he pointed across to the remains of a modest two-storey house. I looked up at the tiny web-covered bedroom window and almost expected to see a young boy, momentarily disturbed from his books, glancing back at us, as if wondering who might be in the haggard.

A CAUTIONARY TALE

An excerpt from John O'Donovan's writings about a legend associated with Kilkenny's Lough Cullen, near his home place. This story documents how the lake was formed.

'A wicked witch wished to destroy a number of young men who were hurling on the plain over which the waters of Lough Cullen spreads itself. One of the hurlers turned off the hurling green (*faithche*) to quench his thirst but not finding any water, he wandered about in search of a well. He was met by the witch in disguise, who told

him that there was no well near at hand but that if he
went over to a tuft of rushes which she pointed out,
and pulled one rush, a well would issue from the earth.
He did what she suggested and forthwith a deluge of
water issued from the earth, which overflowed the plain,
drowned the thirsty youth and all his companions on the
green.'

Buried somewhere within the childhood of many great minds,
you will often find a moment that steered them towards greatness.
For John O'Donovan, a volcanic eruption in Indonesia proved to be
the turning point in his life. Unlikely, but true.

Jim Walsh told me about the massive eruption of Mount
Tambora in 1815, when John O'Donovan was aged about eight. The
event generated an ash cloud so dense that the sun was blacked out.
In effect, there was no summer and consequently no harvest that
year. Hardship and the death of his father saw John move in with
a kindly uncle, Patrick O'Donovan, who offered to support him. It
was during this time that the boy developed a deep love of learning.
His uncle Patrick encouraged his scholarly side, and in time John
became quite the academic and moved to Dublin.

O'Donovan became an authority on folklore, history, place
names and Brehon Law. He also gave lessons in the Irish language.
This, we now know, was how he met Thomas Larcom, director of the
Irish Ordnance Commission, who ultimately offered O'Donovan
the position of Gaelic advisor to the survey. I have little doubt that
the combination of John's natural genius and his humble beginnings
provided the seed bed for the staggering task he accomplished, with
such compassion towards the poor, over the following 10 years.

Starting in Derry, this remarkable place-name pioneer and his
team of linguists worked their way through the entire island of
Ireland, on foot, leaving no marker-stone unturned. They gathered

the minute detail of every one of the almost 63,000 townlands in Ireland. They logged every variation on every name in English and Irish, the meanings, descriptions of the places and the names of all their sources. In the most beautiful penmanship, O'Donovan and his crew recorded a variety of other notes as they went. These very notebooks, which are known as the O'Donovan Name Books, are today stored in the National Archives in Dublin. Despite being two hundred years old, they are perfectly preserved.

When we were filming *Creedon's Atlas of Ireland* for RTÉ, I was fortunate enough to view these notebooks up close. The archivist, Zoe Reid, explained that the field books were all bound with vellum, a type of durable animal skin, possibly pig hide, which protected the notes from wet weather and the passage of time. The pages were made from a form of linen, so were similarly durable. It would appear that information was better protected from the Irish weather than those who collected it!

The National Archives also houses the 'O'Donovan Letters', which he sent back to the survey office while he was on the road. They give remarkable insight into the conditions endured by these place-name pioneers.

As O'Donovan's writing is still legible, I could clearly read the contents of his letters, many of which were peppered with as much wit as they were with detail. His passion for his subject still radiates from the page. Mind you, he wasn't slow to throw a few digs at his employers. He complained about the accommodation and spoke of bed bugs and waking up covered in fleas. He fumed about the innkeepers and landlords, whom he likened to 'a band of respectable robbers', as they were partial, it seems, to increasing the room rate upon realising their guest was a civil servant. Undeterred, O'Donovan and his fellow field workers, who were poorly paid to begin with, gave their all. For example, they often complained of spending their own money on whiskey to loosen tongues as they tried to prise the information from suspicious locals.

By the time the survey finished in 1842, O'Donovan and his team had amassed information on a total of 140,000 place names, including minor place names, like wells, rocky outcrops and the like. If one place name referenced another, that too was documented. Added to all of this, O'Donovan was also the authority when it came to the Irish and English translations, and so he would have suggested the appropriate transliterations in his notes. His paymasters in London needed easy-to-pronounce versions of Irish names, and the Kilkenny man delivered.

ATATEEMORE, COUNTY KILKENNY

Atateemore – Áit an Tí Móir

Áit – Place

Teach (an Tí) – House

Mór (Móir) – Big

Atateemore therefore means 'the place of the big house'.

SLIEVERUE, COUNTY KILKENNY

Slieverue – Sliabh Rua

Sliabh – Hill

Rua – Red

Slieverue therefore means 'the red hill'. I believe the name could be a reference to either the colour of the stone or the vegetation, but there is also a possibility it is a nod to the fern or heather.

LOUGH CULLEN, COUNTY KILKENNY

Lough Cullen – Loch Cuilinn

Loch – Lake

Cuileann (Cuilinn) – Holly

Lough Cullen therefore means 'holly lake'.

SCARTNAMOE, COUNTY KILKENNY
Scartnamoe – Scairt na mBó
Scairt – Undergrowth/thicket/shelter
Bó (na mBó) – of the cows
Scartnamoe therefore can be interpreted as meaning 'the undergrowth of the cows'.

LIFE AFTER THE PLACE NAME SURVEY

The place name survey took up 10 years of O'Donovan's life, much of it spent on the road, away from his wife and children. However, even after he had completed his work on the survey, he never fully left it behind him. He continued to oversee the project and had his expertise called upon frequently. He wrote academic papers on the subject right up until his death.

O'Donovan was just 55 years old when he passed away on 10 December 1861. Three days later, this iconic figure was buried without fuss in the O'Connell Circle of Dublin's Glasnevin Cemetery. He was survived by his wife, Mary Anne Broughton, and six of their nine sons. Ironically, for a man who was so particular about accuracy and detail, there are errors on his headstone. His date of birth is given as 9 July 1809, when in fact he was born on 25 July 1806, while his date of death is given as the day before the actual event!

Inaccuracies aside, I feel it's fitting that he was interred in Glasnevin Cemetery, the final resting place of Daniel O'Connell, Charles Stewart Parnell, Michael Collins and many of Ireland's other patriot dead, for John O'Donovan of Atateemore, County Kilkenny, certainly did his country some service.

9

SAME BUT DIFFERENT

There's an old folk tale that dates from a time when the Russian–Finnish border was being redrawn. Some rather stern officials from Moscow knocked on the door of old Ivan's cabin, which was set in the woods of a disputed territory. They came to enquire whether Ivan and his few acres would be staying within Russia or if Ivan had opted to now give his address as Finland.

'Are you to stay with your old country or will you instead turn your back on us, comrade?' they pressed.

'You know how much I love Mother Russia, my comrades,' Ivan replied, 'and it pains me to have my farm in Finland, but y'know, I am an old man and I fear that even one more Russian winter would kill me.'

Therein lies a great truth. Lines on maps merely define territories; they're geopolitical. They shift and change. Not unlike Ivan, we are all part of an endless continuum, a cultural energy that connects us with our nearest neighbour, irrespective of borders. People grow, old arguments settle, eventually the whole world discovers Italian pizza and the Irish pub. Language doesn't recognise borders. In the Iberian border town of Olivenza, many locals proudly proclaim their Portuguese citizenship, while

Spanish is their language of choice. The mirror-opposite can be found further along the border.

We've already been to the banks of the River Foyle, where the locals refer to the main city as Derry/Londonderry/Doire and the local Derry City FC play all their league matches against teams from across the border in the Republic of Ireland. Limerick–Tipperary hurling rivalries simply melt away when the Munster jerseys emerge from the tunnel at Thomond Park. I guess relationships between next-door neighbours run deepest, for better and for worse.

Over the millennia, Irish relations with our nearest neighbours have been mixed. When we stand back far enough, however, the stories of our two islands are so tightly interwoven, I expect they will never be fully untangled. The history, cultures, peoples, place names and DNA of our people are all so finely entwined, they will never be completely unpicked. It seems as though humans have been programmed to try to get the upper hand over one another since the time of Cain and Abel, and I don't see an end to it in my lifetime. Indeed, as French philosopher Jean-Paul Sartre once said, 'Hell is other people'!

In his 1940s play *No Exit*, Sartre tells the story of three people who die and go to hell. On arrival, they are shown into an empty room and discover that this is where they will spend eternity. No devil, no flames, just the prospect of having to live with each other forever. Indeed, 'Hell is other people'. Why can't they just be like us? Many of the place names of Ireland have implied the very same sentiment for years. The term *an gall* means 'the foreigner' or 'the other' and, generally speaking, it's not a term of endearment. I wonder if non-Irish-speaking members of the former RUC at Donegall Pass police station understood the irony of the place name. It translates as 'the pass at the fortress of the foreigner'. Did Lord Donegall ever stop to consider his fine title and detect the reference to his being 'a stranger in his own lands'?

DONEGAL, COUNTY DONEGAL

Donegal – Dún na nGall

Dún – Fortress

Gaill (na nGall) – (of the) Foreigners

Donegal therefore means 'fortress of the foreigners'.

Apart from County Donegal, there is also a Dún na nGall in County Tipperary and another in County Cork.

MONEYGALL, COUNTY TIPPERARY

Moneygall – Muine Gall

Muine – Thicket

Gaill (Gall) – Foreigners

Moneygall therefore means 'thicket of the foreigners'.

ARDNAGALL, COUNTY GALWAY

Ardnagall – Ard na nGall

Ard – Height, hillock

Gaill (na nGall) – (of the) Foreigners

Ardnagall therefore means 'the hillock of the foreigners'.

BAILE NA NGALL, COUNTY KERRY

There are numerous variations of the name Baile na nGall (townland of the foreigners) – given as Ballynagaul, Ballynagoul, Gaulstown and (curiously) Ballydavid in West Kerry, which maintains its Gaelic name Baile na nGall amongst locals. Place names never forget!

Given the course of Irish history, the term *gall* (plural *gaill*) usually refers to outsiders from Britain, but not exclusively so. Take Fingal in County Dublin, for example. The Irish for Fingal is Fine Gall, meaning 'the foreign tribe'. This is a reference to the Scandinavian foreigners that had settled there.

Here are a few more terms that indicate the presence of outsiders:

▷ *Uiging* is the Gaelicised form of the Old Norse word 'Víkingr'. Dublin's Viking Road, for instance, becomes Bóthar na nUigingeach in Irish.

▷ The Old Irish word for 'Dane' was *Danar*, and is the root of the Dublin place name Bóthar na nDanar, which means 'Dane Road,' or 'Road of the Danes'. *Danar* can even be found in minor place names, such as the very exotic-sounding Timpeallán Chnoc na nDanar in Galway, which means, 'Danes' Hill Roundabout'.

▷ In west County Clare, there is a coastal beauty spot with a name that instantly reveals its historical bounty: Spanish Point. In Irish, the name becomes Rinn na Spáinneach, which means 'headland of the Spaniards'. This is said to refer to part of the Spanish Armada that was wrecked off the west coast of Ireland during the reign of Queen Elizabeth I.

THE HUGUENOTS

In truth, there are many strands to the weave that is 'Irishness'. It's a fabric that is strengthened by its diverse threads. Celt, Dane, Norman and English have all left their mark on the surnames and place names of Ireland. So too have smaller groups. The Huguenots, French Calvinist Protestants, fled persecution in their native France in the 17th and 18th centuries. They settled mainly in Dublin, Cork, Kilkenny, Waterford, Portarlington and Lisburn. Familiar surnames like Cooper, Cox, White, Mullins, King, Britton and Boucher all entered the lexicon of Irish family names. In terms of place names, D'Olier Street in Dublin is named after Jeremiah D'Olier (1745–1817), who was a Huguenot goldsmith, a city sheriff and one of the founders of the Bank of Ireland. Interestingly, he was also a member of the Wide Streets Commission. The commission members clearly felt that Jeremiah was deserving of having one of Dublin's wide streets named after him! French Church Streets in Cork and Portarlington on the Laois/Offaly border are a testament to the Huguenot presence there. Several Huguenot quarters in Irish towns (Galway, Cork, Mallow) boast a Bowling Green Street, which paints a pretty picture of how these French settlers spent their days off.

- -

PORTARLINGTON, COUNTY LAOIS
Portarlington – Cúil an tSúdaire
Cúil – Nook
Súdaire (an tSúdaire) – (of the) tanner/cobbler
The Irish name for Portarlington therefore means 'the nook of the tanner/cobbler'.

- -

LISBURN, COUNTY ANTRIM
Lisburn – Lios na gCearrbhach
Lios – Fort
Cearrbhaigh (na gCearrbhach) – (of the) card players/ gamblers
Lisburn therefore means 'fort of the card players or gamblers'. Just a theory, but the Scots term burn, *meaning 'river', is common all over Ulster, so I'm open to the English version of the place name originating from*

the Irish word lios *and the Scots word* burn, *meaning
'fort of the stream'.*

THE PALATINES

The Palatines were another Protestant group – Lutherans – who fled religious persecution in Germany in 1709. They made it as far as Rotterdam, where, under the orders of Protestant Queen Anne of England, they were rescued by English ships. They were given shelter in England before being invited to take up lands in the British colonies. In Ireland, they settled on lands at Adare and Rathkeale in County Limerick, as well as in counties Kerry, Tipperary and Wexford. Apart from being an act of mercy towards their fellow Protestants, this move was also an attempt by Britain to boost its flagging Protestant population here. The Palatines were not the first, nor the last, wave of refugees to land on Irish shores. However, within a few years, two-thirds of the Palatine community had returned either to Germany or to England. Mind you, in that short time, the Palatines made their mark on the culture of Ireland forever.

Family names that were introduced to Ireland include Fyffe, Glazier, Ruttle and Switzer. Yes, the very same people who gave us Switzers department stores. They also left their mark on the place-names map of Ireland. In County Carlow, for example, there is the village of Palatine (formerly Palatinetown). There are also several references to the group in County Limerick, such as Palatine Bridge near Rathkeale and Rathpalatine a few miles away at Broadford. Dublin meanwhile boasts a Palatine Square. Furthermore, one of the most popular Irish traditional songs is 'Iníon an Phailitínigh', a song in praise of 'The Palatine's Daughter'. Clearly the introduction of such pulchritude into the

Irish gene pool would explain why our crowd are all so good-looking today.

RATHKEALE, COUNTY LIMERICK

Rathkeale – Ráth Caola

Ráth – Fort

Caola – A personal name, perhaps

Rathkeale therefore means 'Caola's fort' (also given as 'Kealy's fort').

RATHPALATINE, COUNTY LIMERICK

Rathpalatine – Ráth na bPalaitíneach

Ráth – Fort

Palaitínigh (na bPalaitíneach) – (of the) Palatines

Rathpalatine therefore means 'the Palatines' fort'.

BROADFORD, COUNTY LIMERICK

Broadford – Béal an Átha

Béal – Mouth

Áth (an Átha) – (of the) Ford

Broadford therefore means 'mouth of the ford'.

Interestingly, Béal an Átha also translates as Ballina, the town in County Mayo. Broadford is a literal translation of an alternative Irish name, An tÁth Leathan, while Ballina is an anglicisation of Béal an Átha.

ADARE, COUNTY LIMERICK

Adare – Áth Dara

Áth – Ford

Dair (Dara) – Oak
Adare therefore means 'ford of the oak'.

GEORGIAN GRANDEUR AND DUBLIN STREET NAMES

Generally speaking, I wouldn't be a great man for the wigs and make-up; however, when Dublin City Tourism offered me the opportunity of being 'A Georgian for a Day', I went for it like make-up was going out of fashion. In Georgian Dublin, it certainly wasn't. Wigs, make-up, lipstick, beauty spots and silk stockings were *de rigueur* for the men as well as the women. So with my buckled shoes, walking cane and three-cornered hat I pranced and paraded myself precociously through the streets of Dublin. Historian Peter Byrne pointed out the fine Georgian façades and the upstairs–downstairs order of the households. Pecking order could be read from the size of the windows, with servants' quarters being at the very top of the house or in the attic.

The Georgian period lasted a little over a hundred years, and was so named because it spanned the reign of four English kings named George. It began with the coronation of King George I of Great Britain and Ireland in 1714 and lasted until the death in 1830 of King George IV. The period is characterised by classical lines in art and architecture, and it gave us those wonderfully symmetrical rows of terraced houses and posh place names that still survive in our large town and cities, particularly Dublin, which was to become the second city of the British Empire.

Dublin's redevelopment was already underway when the first of the Georgian monarchs sat on the throne. Lord Lieutenant of Ireland, the Earl of Ormonde (later made Duke of Ormonde), presided over the development of what was a medieval town, with narrow, winding streets and poor sanitation. Over the centuries the Liffey had developed into little more than an open sewer. Houses backed onto the river, and household waste was simply dumped over the wall into this readymade system that was 'flushed' twice a day by the tide. Ormonde developed the quays that still run along the banks of the river, and he insisted that house-fronts, not rears, should face the river. With the swirl of his quill, Ormonde signed his vision into law and changed the face of Dublin forever. It was to become a capital city to rival many European cities, with its tree-lined quays, neat rows and squares of red-bricked townhouses and classical public buildings, such as the Four Courts and the old Custom House.

Luke Gardiner designed some of Dublin's finest new streets and squares along Dublin's North City, and gave his name to one of the most prominent streets in the area, Gardiner Street. The north side of the city was originally considered far more fashionable than the south side by Dublin Georgians. That was, until the Earl of Kildare decided to build his palatial 'Kildare House' across the city.

'But what about society?' a friend enquired of the earl.

'Where I go, society will follow,' he correctly predicted.

Soon, beautiful Georgian squares were springing up around St Stephen's Green. Kildare Street still bears the earl's name, and Kildare House has since been renamed Leinster House. Yes, the seat of government in Ireland today. During the same period, the Phoenix Park was developed. Despite the reference to classical Greek mythology, the park actually takes its name from the Irish language Páirc an Fhionnuisce. The word *fíonn* means 'bright' or 'clear', and *uisce* means water, so the word 'Phoenix' is merely a colourful and imaginative attempt at *fionnuisce*.

In 1781, at the invitation of John Beresford, who lends his name to Beresford Place, the young master architect James Gandon came to town. His eye for function and beauty gave us the new Custom House, the Four Courts, the King's Inns and Carlisle Bridge, now O'Connell Bridge. He also designed the Irish Houses of Parliament at College Green. Westmoreland Street and Dublin

Castle were also developed at this time. Indeed, Ormond Quay still bears the name of the man who got the whole ball rolling, the Duke of Ormonde.

Grandeur and position were strong social currency, as wealthy Georgians tried to out-do each other. One of the highest compliments was to have a terrace or even an entire street named after you. And so Ireland's elite sprinkled their names around the capital like powder and paint in a Henrietta Street dressing room. The most remarkable example of this vanity goes to Earl Henry Moore of Drogheda, who managed to shoehorn his name into five different Dublin street names, and they are … Earl Street, Henry Street, Moore Street, Of Lane and Drogheda Street (later renamed Sackville Street, and then O'Connell Street). But, 'Of Lane' – I jest you not! Yes, he managed to commemorate himself in five separate addresses. My inner Georgian is swooning at the thought! As a modest man myself, I'd have settled for a simple 'Creedon Close'.

GEORGIAN DUBLIN

Henrietta Street (Sráid Henrietta) – It is believed the street was named after the Duchess of Grafton, Henrietta Fitzroy; however, there is the possibility that it was named in honour of Henrietta Paulet, wife of Charles Paulet, the 2nd Duke of Bolton and Lord Lieutenant of Ireland.

Bolton Steet (Sráid Bolton) – Bolton Street is named after the aforementioned Duke of Bolton, Charles Paulet.

Merrion Square (Cearnóg Mhuirfean) – When the Earl of Kildare/Duke of Leinster elected to have his palatial residence set in Dublin's south side, building what we know today as Leinster House, it resulted in an enormous surge of affluent Georgian townhouses being constructed in the area. Thanks to the influence of the earl, this once-underdeveloped area went from being a relatively undesirable region to having the most beautiful red-brick houses lining its streets and attracting residents from the upper tier of society. Following the construction of Leinster House, three green squares were built, one of which was Merrion Square, named in honour of the Fitzwilliam family, who were Earls of Merrion and integral to its development.

St Stephen's Green (Faiche Stiabhna) – The second of the three squares to be constructed was St Stephen's Green, named in honour of the saintly work carried out by St Stephen. At the time of the park's construction, a nearby church and leprosy hospital also carried the name of the saint. Interestingly, Queen Victoria once requested that the name of the park be changed to Albert Green, in honour of her late husband, Prince Albert. She also proposed that a statue of Prince Albert be erected in the centre of the green. Much to her royal vexation, her idea was rejected.

Fitzwilliam Square (Cearnóg Mhic Liam) – The smallest of Dublin's Georgian squares, Fitzwilliam Square, was developed by, and named after, Richard FitzWilliam, the 7th Viscount FitzWilliam.

GEORGIAN LIMERICK

Pery Square (Cearnóg An Pheirigh) – Pery Square was named in honour of the Anglo-Irish politician Edmund Sexton Pery (also referred to as the Right Honourable Viscount Pery). Given the role he played in the development of Limerick City, it's fitting that a tribute to Viscount Pery was made in the form of a place name.

Henry Street (Sráid Anraí) – Limerick's ever-bustling Henry Street was named in honour of Edmund Henry Pery, the 1st Earl of Limerick and father of the above-mentioned Edmund Sexton Pery. Edmund Sr, who was also known as Lord Glentworth and Viscount Pery, held a seat in the Irish House of Lords.

The Crescent (An Corrán) – While The Crescent takes its current name from the beautiful curvature of the street, it was formerly known as Richmond Place, in honour of the politician and 4th Duke of Richmond Charles Lennox.

Mallow Street (Sráid Mhala) – According to Gerry Joyce's wonderful book on Limerick place names, Mallow Street is named after the Right Rev. William Cecil Pery, who held the title of Baron Glentworth of Mallow.

O'Connell Street (Sráid Uí Chonaill) – While known today as O'Connell Street, named in honour of the political leader Daniel O'Connell, it was formerly known as George's Street, which is said to have been in honour of King George III.

As happened in other Georgian quarters around the then British Empire, some of the finest streets were to slide from society to slum. Red-brick townhouses that were once the boast of Europe became overcrowded tenements by the mid-19th century.

Around the same time, Ireland experienced the inward migration of Jewish refugees, the majority of whom arrived in Dublin in the late 1800s. They were fleeing an anti-Semitic pogrom in Europe, and many settled around Portobello and Camden Street, earning the area the moniker 'Little Jerusalem'. At one stage the area around Clanbrassil Street boasted a large Jewish population, with many kosher shops and bakeries. In more recent years, the Jewish community has for the most part moved to the suburbs or emigrated. Interestingly, this area has since become better known for its mosque than its synagogue. Similarly, Cork City has an area that is still affectionately referred to as Jewtown, and the sign on the local playground reads 'Shalom Park'. Goldsmith and Goldberg still appear in the street names of the city. The community may have dwindled, but our Jewish heritage is safely on the place-names map of Ireland, and through Leopold Bloom in Joyce's *Ulysses*, it also features prominently in Irish literature.

While wigs and silk stockings may have gone out of fashion with the Georgians, the pursuit of power will always be 'in vogue', and the gentrification of place names has never gone away. A 'good address' can add hundreds of thousands of euro to the value of a property. Many wealthy Victorians loved to maintain a British connection in their Irish address, so names like Waterloo, Trafalgar, Windsor and Belgrave all appear on Victorian street names. Native Irish names were considered common by the middle classes, and were often replaced with 'exotic names', as they were known. Italian, French and Spanish place names were supplanted to Ireland as the Dublin middle classes returned from their 'grand tours' with all forms of exotica, animals, plants and place names. They named Sorrento Road and Vico Road in Dalkey after Italian beauty spots. Mind you,

I can appreciate how a Dubliner taking the sea air on Killiney Hill or Dalkey might look out at Dublin Bay and be reminded of the view over the Bay of Naples from the cliffs of Sorrento. That is, until they take off their cardigans! The Cork bourgeoisie favoured Tivoli and Montenotte. Dublin's Portobello was so named to mark a British victory over the Spanish at the Battle of Portobello in Panama. Bellevue, Belleview, Bella Vista and Belvedere all proclaimed the beauty of the view from middle-class Irish mansions in a variety of European languages. As John O'Donovan might have been moved to remark, 'I suppose Áit an Tí Móir wouldn't be grand enough for some of them'.

Places of Catholic pilgrimage like Fatima in Portugal and Lourdes in France also found themselves returning in the suitcases of the devout to be planted forever on the place-names map of Ireland. The hometowns of European saints began to feature in minor place names here, particularly in house names like Lisieux and Assisi. Some are not so obvious, like the Pic du Jer neighbourhood in Cork City, which takes its name from a summit in the Hautes-Pyrénées overlooking Lourdes. I wouldn't have spotted that one in a hurry, but then again, I've often been caught out before. I always assumed that Uam Var Avenue in Bishopstown came from a Dutch name. However, upon enquiry, I discovered it simply comes from the Irish Ascaill na hUaimhe Móire, meaning 'avenue of the big cave'.

- -

BISHOPSTOWN, COUNTY CORK
Bishopstown – Baile an Easpaig
Baile – Townland/town/home
Easpag (an Easpaig) – (of the) Bishop
Bishopstown therefore means 'the town of the bishop'.

KILLINEY, COUNTY DUBLIN
Killiney – Cill Iníon Léinín
Cill – Church
Iníon Léinín – Léinín's daughter
Killiney therefore means 'church of the daughter
of Léinín'.

DALKEY, COUNTY DUBLIN
Dalkey – Deilginis
Deilginis – Thorn Island
Dealg is the Irish for 'thorn' and ey is the Old Norse
Viking word for 'island'.

There are so many terms to describe streets and features on the urban landscape, and it can be great fun to try and crack the code. Take a look through the glossary at the back of the book; it will help you piece together the real meaning behind your own local *logainmneacha*. I recently came across a little terrace named Bailtín Chathail, which is also given as Cahill Ville on the street sign. However, with a little imagination, it could also be given as Charleville, or 'little home of Cathal'.

THE FEELING BEHIND THE NAME

I was travelling by bus in Poland one day when I tried to rest my head against the window. However, the vibration of the engine rattled the glass at my ear, ensuring there would be no sleep. I was daydreaming when a sign suddenly came into view. It read 'Auschwitz'. The word itself felt like a blow to the chest. Even though I was part of a group going to pay our respects at the former Nazi death camp, seeing the name in print knocked me for six. I can only imagine the pain that still aches in the hearts of the millions of people directly affected by that place.

I've come to appreciate the emotional pressure that is encased in some place names. Chernobyl, Hiroshima and Nagasaki were all just the names of towns once, until injected with an energy so awful that it radiates forever from their names. It's not uncommon for victims to have a physiological reaction to the name of the place where the trauma occurred.

We have many *logainmneacha* in Ireland that are similarly imbued with trauma. Many find it hard to utter the place names Omagh and Enniskillen without thinking of the people who lost their lives there. Crossmaglen, the Bogside and so many more place names in Northern Ireland are forever associated with the Troubles. Many of my generation find it difficult to say 'Kingsmill' without silently adding the word 'massacre'.

South of the border, we too have our share of pain. I expect most of us can think of a place name that invokes a pang every time we encounter it. Killeen/An Cillín is a common *logainm* that often refers to a location where stillborn or unbaptised children were buried. The name is infused with heartache, and there are many dotted around the country.

I recall a trip to Inis Oírr some years ago. I swapped stories and craic with a man and his children on the ferry back to Doolin. He was teasing me about the poor form the Cork hurlers were showing that summer. When I asked him, 'Where are you from yourself?' his smile dropped, and he whispered something apologetically.

'Sorry, where?' I said.

He quietly repeated his earlier response, 'Letterfrack.'

The mood became more sombre as we reflected on the terrible regime that prevailed at the industrial school there. We spoke about the meaning of the name – from the Irish Leitir Fraic, meaning 'speckled hill'. I noted the fact that the village was founded during the Great Famine by Quakers, who had dispensed great charity and relief to the local people. He acknowledged the fact, but said that all the good was overshadowed by the terrible injustice meted out at the industrial school. 'Whenever we say where we're from, it's the only thing people want to talk about. It's not their fault. It's just the whole thing is so bloody awful.'

We spoke about the holidays and hurling again.

There is power in a place name, and it's not always benign. There have been many attempts to lose the pain in translation. Ballybough in Dublin began life as An Baile Bocht, meaning 'the poor town'. Similarly, the Cork suburb of Mayfield also appeared on the double-decker buses of my childhood as 'Baile na mBocht' *as Gaeilge*, in this case meaning 'townland of the poor'. The more up-to-date translation of Mayfield is now Gort Álainn, meaning 'lovely field'.

When I visited the National Archives of Ireland in Dublin to view John O'Donovan's collection of notebooks, I was determined not to leave without finding the meaning behind one particular place name that had puzzled me for years: Gortnalour. It was a place my father had often spoken about, and as an adult I had encountered it myself while hillwalking on Shehy Mountain.

- -
SHEHY MOUNTAIN, GLENA, COUNTY KERRY
Shehy Mountain – Cnoc na Seithe
Cnoc – Hill
Seithe (na Seithe) – Animal hide
Shehy Mountain therefore means 'the hill of the animal hide'.

The word *gort* usually means 'a field', so when coupled with the word *leabhar*, which is Irish for 'book', I felt the translation might be along the lines of 'the field of the books'. Maybe there was a hedge school there at one stage? The presence of an old run-down schoolhouse in nearby Tooreenalour further supported my theory that it might once have been a place of education.

After all, the word *tor* is Irish for 'bush', so *torín* would be 'a little bush', surely. Put it all together and you have 'the small bush of the books', further implying the presence of a hedge school in the area. With these two places being in such close proximity, and with every clue pointing towards that of a hedge school, I was convinced I had cracked the code. Not so, it seems!

When I looked into both of these places in the National Archives, I discovered I was very wrong. The word I had assumed was *leabhar*, meaning 'book', was actually *lobhar*, meaning 'leper'. Gortnalabhar translated as 'the field of the lepers', while Tooreenalour became Tuairín na Lobhar, meaning 'little pasture of the lepers'. On further investigation, I discovered that the place name was recorded there as early as 1584. Leprosy was one of the most common and virulent diseases in medieval Ireland. Bubonic plague and smallpox also were often referred to as leprosy, and the infected would be cast out from centres of population. I shudder to think of the poor outcasts whose misery is etched forever in the place names of my own *áit dúchais*.

Sadly, I found accounts of similarly wretched souls hidden in place names all over our country. One that will come as a great surprise to many is Leopardstown (Baile na Lobhar). This was originally known as Leperstown but, over the course of time, was amended slightly to its current name.

I remember spotting a street sign over one of Cork's most exclusive addresses; it states 'Lover's Walk'. The Irish translation beneath reads, 'Siúl na Lobhar', meaning 'walk of the lepers'. Its location at the edge of the city would support its use as a point of 'no entry'. It transpires there was a leprosarium for the infected in the nearby village of Glanmire, and so a sentry was placed at the high ground here, on the approach the city.

CLOONALOUR, TRALEE, COUNTY KERRY

Cloonalour – Cluain na Lobhar

Cluain – Meadow (cluain can also mean 'wet pasture')

Lobhair (na Lobhar) – (of the) Lepers

Cloonalour therefore means 'meadow of the lepers'.

KNOCKNALOUR, KILRUSH, COUNTY WEXFORD

Knocknalour – Cnoc na Lobhra

Cnoc – Hill

Lobhair (na Lobhra) – (of the) Lepers

Knocknalour therefore means 'the hill of the lepers'.

RATHNALOUR, NEWCHAPEL, COUNTY TIPPERARY

Rathnalour – Ráth na Lobhar

Ráth – Fort

Lobhair (na Lobhar) – (of the) Lepers

Rathnalour therefore means 'lepers' fort', or 'fort of the lepers'.

DROMALOUR, DROMTARRIFF, COUNTY CORK

Dromalour – Drom an Lobhair

Droim – Ridge

Lobhair (na Lobhar) – (of the) Lepers

The full address therefore means 'lepers' ridge at bull's ridge'.

Another place thought to be connected to the leprosy plague is Dublin's Misery Hill. It is located quite close to the former site of a leprosy hospital and, apparently, leprosy sufferers would be walked to the hospital accompanied by a man ringing a bell and another carrying a 40-foot pole to keep members of the public at a safe distance from the sick. The Dublin City Council website cites this as the origin of the expression, 'I wouldn't touch him with a 40-foot pole!' Given the association of the disease with Misery Hill, it would certainly explain why the area is sometimes referred to locally as 'Lepers' Hill'.

The historical origins of the place name are said to go back to the days when the bodies of those executed at Gallows Hill were hauled over to Misery Hill and publicly displayed for quite some time as a warning to others tempted to stray from the straight and narrow.

LEPROUS LEOPARDS

In the 14th century, a leprosy hospital was built in modern-day Leopardstown (Baile na Lobhar).

TIPPERARY'S BOATE AND HEMSWORTH FAMILIES

Back in the 16th century, a number of professionals rather vocally attributed the eating habits of the Irish to the origins of our virulent plague of leprosy. Insufficient boiling and roasting of meat were thought to produce fluids that caused leprosy when ingested. Likewise, the widespread consumption of uncooked fish was also thought to have played a role. In his hugely fascinating book *The Leper Hospitals of Munster*, author Gerard A. Lee quotes Dr Gerard Boate's belief that leprosy was 'the fault and foul gluttony of the inhabitants, in the successive devouring of unwholesome salmons'.

I looked up Dr Boate after I read his quote, and of course this brought me down another rabbit hole – one I only managed to burrow back out of after an hour had flown by! Dr Boate, I read, was none other than the chief physician to Cromwell's army. Some 17 years after his death in 1650, his widow Katherine Menning was given over one thousand acres of forfeited land in Tipperary as a gesture of thanks for Dr Boate's generous monetary contributions towards the suppression of the Irish rebellion. While the Boate family remained in Tipperary for a number of generations, the marriage of Dr Boate's great-granddaughter, Lucy Boate, to the Vicar of Birr, Rev. William Hemsworth, meant the land subsequently came under the ownership of the Hemsworth family.

PIPERSTOWN

Abbeville, the name given to the Hemsworth seat of residence in Tipperary, formerly Piperstown, is Baile an Phíobaire in Irish, meaning 'home of the piper'. A wonderful contrast between the two cultures that consider the place home.

10

THE FINAL WORD

The pilot's voice crackles something about preparing for our final descent, and an excited fidgeting spreads through the cabin. Like the boy in the row in front of me, I lean my cheek firmly against the window to catch my first glimpse of Ireland, just as I strained to catch the first sight of Kit and Jack's house whenever we passed Johnny the Cross's shop, on the way to Adrigole. Every little boy the world over has always known that his mother is the most beautiful in the world. I gaze down at her hills and clouds. I just can't stop myself smiling. She's still here, just as I left her, like a steady and loving mother. I can't wait to lose myself in her cardigan of green. I could never visualise the land of my birth as 'the fatherland'. No, for me, Ireland will always be female – my motherland. It's just how I've always seen her. Countless generations of Irish have felt something similar. It's what makes us all family, I suppose. We all share a common motherland. I think of all those before us who had to say goodbye while clutching a one-way ticket. A final glance over the shoulder and then countless nights in a foreign bedroom longing for the sound of her voice.

Like all adult children, there comes a time when you lose a parent, and you begin to realise that they too were young once. It can happen at a funeral when one of their contemporaries speaks of them by an unfamiliar name, a nickname that only existed in a now silent schoolyard. Like the old song says, 'You'll never miss your mother 'til she's gone.' In my own case, absence has made the heart grow fond and the mind grow curious. It's had me search the genealogical records for information about Blakes and Creedons long since gone to their rest. All of my ancestors, right down to my last aunt and uncle, have now departed the stage. Did any of them look like my own children and grandchildren? Were the Creedons always talkers? There's a growing urgency to my search. Time is moving on. I'm already losing family members of my own generation and there's no stop-button on this conveyor belt.

My relationship with Mother Ireland feels something similar. I dearly want to know more about her and what she was like when she was younger and our ancestors wrote songs in praise of her beauty. What did they call her before she became Ireland?

My enquiries led me to a wonderful day on Ireland's Eye in the company of linguistics expert Dr Anna Pytlowany from Poland and Professor David Stifter from Austria, who is Professor of Old Irish at Maynooth University. David took me through Ptolemy's view of Ireland and the etymology of the name 'Ireland'. Amongst other things, I discovered that an Italian map in the 1400s referred to Britain and Ireland collectively as 'Britain'. A very early variant of the term 'British Isles' dates from Ancient Greece, when these neighbouring isles were referred to as the 'Pretanic Islands'. So perhaps the term didn't originate in London, but on the sailing maps and charts of Mediterranean powers who simply lumped us together as a couple of cold, wet islands in the north-western corner of the world. Either way, I've never warmed to the term 'British Isles'. Good fences make good neighbours after all.

So how did Ireland's name evolve? Professor Stifter explained that while Pytheas, the Greek explorer, gave the name of the island as 'Ierne', Proto-Celts (*proto* meaning 'first' or 'earliest', as in 'prototype') referred to the island as Φῑwerjon, which translates as 'abundant one' and includes 'Φiwer', a variation on the ancient Sanskrit word *pivan*, meaning 'plump, fertile or abundant'. Ptolemy's map, around a hundred years after the crucifixion of Christ, gave it as 'Iouernia'. The Romans offered the similar-sounding 'Hibernia', meaning 'land of winter' in Latin. I expect their advance parties might have been looking for an excuse not to advance any further, and baulked at the Irish weather. Remember, they had a bags of a time trying to conquer the Picts in the north of Britain. Indeed, it came to the point there where they gave up, built Hadrian's Wall and literally drew a line under it, creating what became modern-day Scotland.

The native Irish named this island after the Celtic Goddess Ériu, which in time became Éire (Éirinn in the dative, as in Erin go Bragh, and Éireann in the genitive, as in Dáil Éireann). Ériu was a matronly figure and had two sisters, Banba and Fódla. Mythology says that when the Milesians first arrived on these shores, all three sisters asked that their name be given to the land. Ériu became the most prevalent, but her two sisters have also made a few guest appearances.

Banba and Fódla were to lend their names when the native Irish were forbidden to utter the name of their country. When all references to Éire/Éireann were outlawed, Banba became the secret replacement name for those who wished to maintain their ancient connection to the land. Poets have drawn on a variety of female names, including the beautiful Róisín Dubh (Dark Rosaleen), but Ériu/Éire has prevailed. Neighbouring Celtic languages also do it justice. In Scottish Gaelic, it's referred to as 'Eirinn' and it appears in Manx as 'Nerin'. Interestingly, Nerin is another fine example of removing the first letter – the 'a' in the definite article – and sliding the solitary 'n' over to join the vowel of the next word. We also see this with 'An Uaimh' becoming Navan and 'An Obair' becoming Nobber, both in County Meath, and 'An Aill' emerging as 'Naul' in North County Dublin.

NAVAN, COUNTY MEATH
Navan – An Uaimh
An Uaimh – The cave
Navan literally translates as 'the cave'.

NOBBER, COUNTY MEATH
Nobber – An Obair
An Obair – The work
Nobber simply means 'the work'. It got the name
when Normans were building the castle there
and work was plentiful for locals. So, in effect,
Nobber takes its name from the building boom
there in the 13th century.

THE NAUL, COUNTY DUBLIN
(The) Naul – An Aill
An Aill – The cliff
Naul means 'the cliff', while 'the Naul' means
'the the cliff'!

The English name 'Ireland' is a compound of the Irish name Ériu and the English word 'land', which has its roots in Germanic and Old Norse languages. Interesting that Ériu was seen by the early Celts as 'abundant one', and was also personified as 'a matronly figure' by them. That's exactly how it was viewed in the late 20th century by me, as I coloured in the map of Ireland on the back-cover of my copybook. In fact, I'm a little relieved that I wasn't the first to see the mammy in Ireland.

THE EVOLUTION OF IRELAND'S NAMES

Proto-Celtic – Φīwerjon

Proto-Goidelic – Īweriū

Old Irish – Ériu

Modern Irish – Éire

When the Anglo-Irish Treaty was signed in December 1921, the War of Independence came to an end. The following year, 26 of Ireland's counties became a dominion of the British Commonwealth, to be known as Saorstát na hÉireann, or Irish Free State in the English language. The remaining six counties were to be known as Northern Ireland, and would remain within the United Kingdom. By 1931, the British Parliament began to relinquish authority over all its dominions. The Irish Free State was to become the first of the former dominions to be internationally recognised as a fully sovereign state. Having abolished the oath of allegiance to the Crown, the next step in the decoupling from Britain was the introduction, in 1937, of Bunreacht na hÉireann, the Irish Constitution. This was to be a significant step in the birth of a nation and the evolution of its place name. Henceforth, the country was to be known in the 'first official language' as Éire, and would be named 'Ireland' in the English language.

Britain refused to accept the English version of the state's name. It regarded the use of the generic 'Ireland' by the government in Dublin as a clear indication of its claim to sovereignty over the entire island. It was also a source of outrage to the Loyalist population in the remaining six counties of Northern Ireland.

This came to a head at the Olympic Games of 1948. The summer games were hosted by England, and the opening ceremony would see the team from each participating country march behind a banner bearing the English-language version of that country's name. So, Italia would march behind a banner reading 'Italy', and so on. Thus, the Olympic Council of Ireland decided that the Irish team, already torn by North/South differences, would walk behind a banner bearing the name 'Ireland'. Lord Burghley, head of the organising committee in London, wouldn't hear of it. The name 'Ireland' wasn't recognised by the British. But a compromise had to be reached. As a result, the Irish contingent would be the only visitors at the opening ceremony to march behind a banner sporting their own language. They trooped around a packed Wembley Stadium behind a banner bearing the name 'Éire' and were placed in alphabetical order between Egypt and Finland. I can only imagine the conversations in the VIP box …

'I say. Éire, where's that?'

'Somewhere between Egypt and Finland. Milesians, I believe.'

Later that year, on 21 December 1948, an Act of the Oireachtas/Government declared the country would now become known as the Republic of Ireland. Significantly, this act also removed from the British monarchy all authority in Ireland. Eventually, with the signing of the Good Friday Agreement at Hillsborough in 1998, the British parliament repealed the Government of Ireland Act of 1920, which had asserted territorial rights over all of Ireland. The electorate in the Republic of Ireland voted to remove Articles 2 and 3 of the Irish Constitution which asserted a territorial claim over Northern Ireland.

Alastair Campbell, who was key to the negotiations, returned to Hillsborough and walked the gardens with me for our *Creedon's Road Less Travelled* series. We spoke about the long and often fractious relationship between our two islands and the delicate nature of peace. I came away in the knowledge that we shouldn't be surprised if borders shift again. The English have voted to leave the EU. Northern Ireland voted against Brexit and so too did Scotland. Who knows what the future might bring?

SÍNEADH FADA

You may occasionally encounter a road sign in Ireland where the letters are unintelligible. You are not alone. Most Irish speakers under the age of 70 would have some difficulty deciphering such a sign. What you are looking at here is a Gaelic script known as An Cló Gaelach. Evolving from Latin, it was originally used in medieval manuscripts and had an 18-letter alphabet. Cló Gaelach first appeared as the printed word in 1571 in Seán Ó Cearnaigh's book *Aibidil Gaoidheilge agus Caiticiosma* (*Irish Alphabet and Catechism*). That typeface remained in use until the 1960s. Indeed, a version of the typeface was developed for computers by Ciarán Ó Duibhín.

My older siblings were schooled in this script. I wasn't. I remember parents bemoaning the change to Roman script, not only because it severed a link to a language that had endured for generations, but it also meant an end to the hand-me-down schoolbooks for a while! The old script still survives on a handful of street signs and post boxes that I hope will be preserved. It also appears on the official seal of An Garda Síochána.

I remember the mid-1970s, when Ireland was modernising at a fantastic rate. The country now had its own airports and the rural electrification scheme had finally lit even the Black Valley in County Kerry (Com Uí Dhuibh, meaning 'black glen'). The country had recently joined the EEC, forerunner to the EU, and a new decimal currency had been introduced. However, when rumour spread that the *síneadh fada* would be the next to go, there was uproar. It began in 1974, when the Department of Posts and Telegraphs issued a new series of stamps bearing the word 'Eire'. Did you see that? There's the *síneadh fada* gone! It didn't take long before the missing accent was spotted. Noel Davern, TD for Tipperary South, led the charge and raised the matter in the Dáil.

'Where is our *síneadh fada*?' he thundered. 'We demand its immediate restoration.'

The argument was dismissed by the then Minister for Posts and Telegraphs, Conor Cruise O'Brien, who pointed out that the *fada* had been gone 10 years. He also added that the practice of printing signage in Roman script, without the accents, was already standard in several European languages, including French. Minister O'Brien further made the case that the *fada* had to be removed from the stamp for 'artistic balance'. The division only deepened. Would we really erase part of our heritage to follow fashion in some effort to be perceived as modern?

Davern delivered the decisive blow when he pointed out that spelling Éire without the fada was worse than a misspelling. The TD explained that the word on the stamp did not even mean Ireland. The fada is what determines the pronunciation as 'ae-ra'. It also determines its meaning. Without the *fada* on the first letter 'e', this word, *eire*, means 'a burden, a load or an encumbrance'.

The minister replied that it didn't mean 'encumbrance' to anyone except Mr Davern. Fortunately, tradition won the day, and our stamps later reverted to the Gaelic type and the *síneadh fada* was restored. I take my hat off to Noel Davern, the Tipperary man who went to battle 'in the name of the *fada*'.

WHERE HAS OUR FIFTH PROVINCE GONE?

Today the island of Ireland is made up of four provinces, yet the Irish word for a province is *cúige*, meaning 'a fifth'. This fact often requires a double take. Literally, it suggests we are only four-fifths of what we used to be. So where is our missing province? Has it too been sacrificed to modernity, like they tried to do to our poor *síneadh fada*? Not quite, but it did disappear with the unstoppable march of time. The missing province is Mide, which loosely translates as 'middle', for indeed it was right in the middle of Ireland. Mide existed for over a millennium, from the first century to the 12th century, and was located roughly where Meath and Westmeath are today. Indeed, the names of those two counties clearly have their roots in the old province.

Mide also included parts of modern-day counties Louth, Cavan, Longford, Dublin, Kildare and Offaly. Although the smallest of the five provinces, Mide was hugely influential, being home to the High King of Ireland in Tara. With the passage of time and the arrival of the Normans, it was inevitable that power would eventually shift. In 1172, the kingdom was awarded to Hugh de Lacy, who acquired the title Lordship of Meath. In 1610, the English parliament set the boundaries of the four existing provinces. Cavan reverted to Ulster, and what was left of Mide was absorbed into Leinster. The boundaries haven't shifted since.

These days, the provinces serve no administrative role and exist purely as cultural regions. In my lifetime, however, I have seen our sense of 'provincehood' fall, then rise again. For example, Cumann Lúthchleas Gael/the Gaelic Athletic Association has maintained the tradition of four inter-county provincial championships providing the basis for an All-Ireland Championship. However, the once hugely popular Railway Cup competitions, in which four teams – each selected from within a province – would compete for the trophy, was eventually abandoned in 2017 after Connaught pulled out. They cited, amongst other things, lack of spectator interest.

On the other hand, the rise in popularity of rugby in this country has seen a reawakening of our once intense love of province. The establishment of the European Rugby Champions Cup, also known as the Heineken Cup, provided the spark. While Ireland didn't have rugby clubs strong enough to compete with the big British and French clubs, we did have a provincial structure that might. So the four provinces of Ireland were accepted into the competition and have done particularly well. Men and women from rival counties, who would normally be on opposite sides of a football or hurling match, now find themselves standing shoulder to shoulder, waving their provincial colours.

In simple terms, a province is a kingdom. We once had many provinces, but how did the surviving four get their names? Like many ancient place names, they simply identify the people who lived there. If you look at Ptolemy's map, there are 47 words on it, and most of them refer to the tribe that held sway in the area. The province names date from the Gaelic period. The prefix, or first part, in each name identifies the dominant tribe. The '-ster' suffix means 'territory of', and derives from the Old Norse word *staor*.

For the most part, Vikings landed in three of our provinces, resulting in the '-ster' suffix in the words Munster, Leinster and Ulster. The name Connaught, however, displays no Viking influence, and is formed purely from a sept/tribal name. The people of Connaught were the descendants of Conn.

ULSTER – Cúige Uladh
Given that cúige means province, and Ulaidh is the ancient name of the Ulidians or Ulstermen, we can deduce that the name Ulster means 'province of the Ulaidh'.

LEINSTER – Cúige Laighean
Laighnigh is the Modern Irish for Laigin, the name of a tribe that occupied the area. Cúige Laighean, therefore, means 'province of the Laighnigh or people of Laigin'.

CONNAUGHT – Cúige Chonnacht

Connachta is a reference to the mythical king Conn Cétchathach (Con of the Hundred Battles). Knowing this, we can see that the Irish term for Connaught – Cúige Chonnacht – translates into English as 'province of the descendants of Conn'.

MUNSTER – Cúige Mumhan

The name Muma (later Mumha, currently 'an Mumhain') for Munster is cited in the Annals of the Four Masters as having been derived from that of the High King, Eocaidh Mumho. This suggests that 'Munster' therefore means 'province, or kingdom, of Mumho'.

COUNTIES

Within the four existing provinces we have 32 counties. The concept of a county arrived here with the Normans in the 12th century and took almost four hundred years to fully establish. In essence, a county was an administrative unit created to enforce tax, security and justice at a local level. Like the provinces, many of the Irish counties take their names from the ruling tribes. For example, Offaly is Uíbh Fhailí, which is derived from Uí Fhailge, the dominant group in that region. Similarly, Tyrone is an anglicised transliteration of Tír Eoghain, which translates as 'Eoghan's land', while Tír Chonaill, meaning 'Conall's territory', is better known now as County Donegal.

Lovers of Gaelic games might enjoy the irony in the fact that the county is a concept imported from Britain, given that we are probably at our most Gaelic at inter-county games. Toponymy is a millefeuille, with many layers. Apart from the provinces and counties

THAT PLACE WE CALL HOME

of Ireland, we have about 300 baronies, which were introduced here during the conquest of Ireland in the 16th century. Like ecclesiastical dioceses, many of them overlap county boundaries. Next we have over 2,000 civil parishes, plus local electoral districts, towns, villages, about 50,000 street names and of course the 63,000 townlands. Furthermore, within the townlands there are the countless field names, streams, hills, ancient monuments and other minor place names, each one offering another tiny particle of insight into the story of the land and the people who once walked it.

Increasingly, people are again walking the townlands of Ireland. I have encountered numerous community groups conducting local field-name surveys. Over the past seven years, John McCullen and the 400 members of the Meath Fields Project have logged almost 30,000 names. The Westmeath survey has also made considerable progress in gathering the field names of the county lest they disappear under the tarmac of motorways and other developments and are lost forever. Most of the names are predictable, the house field, the bog field, the shed field and so on. Others, however, tell a bigger tale, like 'Cromwell's Bush' and 'Cromwell's Cross', field names that date from the Siege of Drogheda. I also once encountered 'Sarsfield's Ride' on a road outside Limerick City. (The funny thing about this one is that I was there to play a small part in the television comedy *Killinaskully*, which is actually filmed in a place called Killoscully, which could be interpreted as meaning 'church of the scholar'.)

HOW DID OUR NAMES GET ON THEIR MAPS?

For many centuries, the Irish have emigrated in huge numbers. Mass transportation to the penal colonies, the Great Famine of the 1840s and subsequent economic downturns have seen literally millions of people leave this island never to return. Some would bring a stone from the home place in their pocket as a keepsake; others brought songs and stories. Words like 'craic', 'boycott', 'shenanigans' and even the place name 'Blarney' emigrated with us and entered the language of our adoptive homes.

There are several Limericks, Dublins and Tipperarys around the world. Listowel is out there too. There's a Tyrone, Waterford and Westmeath in Ontario, and a Wicklow in New Brunswick. There's a Port Erin on the Isle of Man, and in Papua New Guinea you'll find an island called New Ireland. Would you believe there's a Glendalough State Park in Minnesota and a Mullingar in Saskatchewan, Canada? I expect my GPS would make perfect sense out there when it pronounces 'Mullingar' as 'Moolinger'.

I once encountered a little place in Somerset, in England, called Beckery. I discovered it comes from the Old Irish word *bec*, meaning 'small', and 'Ériu', the ancient word for Ireland. So Beckery means 'Little Ireland', and it's believed locally that an Irish man, possibly a slave, was left there by the Vikings to tend to their longphort, and so it became known as 'Little Ireland' in the old language. This might have been the same exchange programme that saw St Patrick land on these shores some years earlier.

Virtually every town and village in Ireland is represented abroad, but the one *logainm* that has really punched above its weight is the little village of Avoca. There are 13 Avocas in the US alone, with many more in Australia and around the world. It has lent its name to towns, villages, farms, school districts and more. The reason the name Avoca travelled so well is due largely to the song 'The Meeting of the Waters' by Thomas Moore. Moore's melodies were hugely popular in the parlour society of the 1800s, and 'The Meeting of the Waters' sang the praises of Avoca. Typically, it was sung by men in moustaches, with an elbow on the mantelpiece and an eye on the young lady accompanying him at the piano.

Soon after, the gramophone was invented. Its arrival was, in effect, the beginning of mass media. For the first time, music or speech could be recorded and disseminated on a mass scale. The gramophone was to music what the printing press was to books. The time was ripe for Avoca to take its place among the great nations of the Earth. Irish tenor John McCormack was all the rage in the early 1900s, and so too was the music of Thomas Moore. So when recordings of McCormack singing 'The Meeting of the Waters' were played at social gatherings all over the English-speaking world, people fell in love with the beautiful imagery and the soft sound of Avoca. It didn't take long before misty-eyed Irish emigrants were naming their new homes after a little spot that first appeared on Ptolemy's map a couple of millennia earlier. The gramophone records sold by the shipload; Avoca had gone viral!

Many Irish convicts were transported to the colonies to fulfil labour requirements. I remember a guide at the 19th-century penal settlement at Port Arthur in Tasmania telling us that sentences were often handed down to meet British needs overseas. In other words, if you were unskilled or elderly, you might get a week in prison or six lashes for stealing a bag of apples. But if you were a skilled labourer found guilty of the same crime, you would more likely be sent on a convict ship to the colonies, where you would be put to work developing British settlements there. This practice saw many Irishmen and women shuffle down gangplanks all over the British Empire.

The Caribbean colonies were no exception. St Patrick and the Irish saints are well represented on the map of Jamaica. The people of Cork in particular have fed into the culture, accent and place names of Montserrat. Indeed, I remember the Irish television series *Radharc* made a wonderful programme on that island in the early 1970s. It featured an elderly Afro-Caribbean couple at their home in the township of Kinsale. There was a shamrock over the door, and the *fear an tí* sang 'Mother Machree', another John McCormack classic, in a beautiful broad Cork accent. He was no John McCormack, but he certainly left me misty-eyed and mystified.

Not far from Kinsale in Montserrat, you'll find a place called Cork Hill, and there's no shortage of McCarthys in the Montserrat phone book. I remember when I was trekking in the hills near Tamil Nadu in India, I came around the corner and got a right land when, there in the approach to a vast tea plantation, a huge sign greeted me, saying 'Welcome to Connemara'. Like Hansel and Gretel dropping breadcrumbs, it's as though emigrants from all nations drop a trail of place names as they go, as if it might help them navigate a way home.

But why limit place naming to planet Earth? Why not go into the universe itself? Well, that we did, and as a result, there is a place called Tara on Mars. I jest you not. I even saw it for myself when visiting the European Space Agency near Frascati in Italy to film an item about weather satellites. Fair enough, as place names go, Frascati sounds cool and exotic, but hey, Ireland has a *logainm* on Mars!

In fact, I discovered that many Irish names have found themselves headed in the general direction of the final frontier. For example, also on Mars, there's the Louth Crater, Navan Crater, Glendore Crater, Lismore Crater, and a Wicklow Crater. That's a lot of lonely craters with only each other for company. There's also a vast area called the 'Connemara Chaos Zone' in the Europa constellation. So now! Let that be an eye-opener to anyone who thought the Connemara Chaos Zone was a house party in the West of Ireland.

THE FUNNY, THE RUDE AND THE QUIRKY – IRELAND'S UNUSUAL PLACE NAMES

LUCKY LANE – STONEYBATTER, COUNTY DUBLIN

Now this is an address we'd all like to have! It transpires that the name came about after locals shared some stories with architect Peter Carroll. In an *Irish Independent* article, Peter recalled how, when he was trying to come up with a name for the street, he canvassed elderly locals from the street and asked if they had any stories about the place. A number of ladies told him it used to be known as Lucky Lane, and shared with him some anecdotes that inspired the nickname. That nickname is now official!

LADIES VIEW – KILLARNEY, COUNTY KERRY
When Queen Victoria visited Killarney back in 1861, her ladies-in-waiting visited a particularly scenic viewpoint. They were so mesmerised by the beautiful vista that it was named after them.

ATMOSPHERIC ROAD – DALKEY, COUNTY DUBLIN
No doubt many a tourist has done a double take when passing this place-name sign! The origins of Dalkey's Atmospheric Road lie in the presence of the Atmospheric Railway, which ran in the area.

BALLYDEHOB – SCHULL, COUNTY CORK
If it didn't already exist, you'd swear the name Ballydehob had been dreamt up by an American movie producer looking to name an Irish location in a film. *As Gaeilge*, Ballydehob is Béal Átha an Dá Chab, which means 'mouth of the river with two openings'.

MOLL'S GAP – KILLARNEY, COUNTY KERRY
The famous Moll's Gap is actually named after Kerry woman Moll Kissane, who ran a shebeen there in which she sold poitín. Prior to being named after Moll, it was named 'Céim an Daimh', meaning 'the Ox's step'.

HACKBALLSCROSS – DUNDALK, COUNTY LOUTH
There's a lot of uncertainty surrounding the origins of this unusual village moniker. Legend and lore, however, seem to suggest that an 18th-century landlord gruesomely hacked a number of thieves to death after finding them on his property. The Irish name, Crois an Mhaoir, translates as 'the steward's/warden's cross/crossroads'.

BASTARDSTOWN – KILMORE, COUNTY WEXFORD

Well here's one that never fails to make it onto every list of 'unusual Irish place names'. The Wexford townland of Bastardstown, or Baile Bhastaird as it becomes *as Gaeilge*, refers to the homestead of the Anglo-Norman Bastard family. It may sound like a highly unusual surname in this day and age; however, it was actually quite common at one time.

CRAZY CORNER – MULLINGAR, WESTMEATH

This was a tough one to crack. Type the name into Google and you will be greeted by countless results comprising mainly Airbnb listings that are interrupted by a web page containing the coordinates for Crazy Corner, and one line that just reads, 'Yes this is its actual name!' It was only when I came across Paul Clements' book *The Height of Nonsense: The Ultimate Irish Road Trip* that I finally discovered how such a name came about. According to a local man, a blacksmith forge was once situated in the now derelict building at the corner. The blacksmith's name was Gracey, so naturally it became known as Gracey's Corner. Such is the everchanging nature of language, Gracey's Corner over time became distorted to 'Crazy Corner', which has since become its official name.

DOODY'S BOTTOMS – DONARD, COUNTY WICKLOW

No one seems to know exactly why this townland was given this name, but there is a tiny clue to be found within the archived records of the Place Names Branch. A note dated 1839 was accompanied by the code [OD:AL] followed by the text:

'ODowda's bottom land' [OD Nóta]

The OD being referenced in the records is none other than the famous John O'Donovan! That was his note! Many Irish farms still have a field at the bottom of an incline known as 'the bottoms'. I encountered a few of these myself in Meath and Westmeath. But, as bad as 'Doody's Bottoms' may sound, it's no match for the London's Pratt's Bottom, situated on the border with Kent.

PAPS OF ANU – KILLARNEY, COUNTY KERRY

I'm not entirely sure who it was that first looked up at these twin hills one day and suddenly decided they not only looked like breasts but that the cairn of stones at the very top of each hill resembled nipples … well, whoever they were, they evidently shared their findings, because the nickname 'The Paps of Anu' remains to this day! The Anu being credited with said 'paps' was actually an ancient Irish goddess. No doubt she's delighted with her landscape legacy!

BUILD AND REBUILD

Like language itself, place names are organic. They are created, they exist and quite often they die. Some of our older place names were first spoken in languages now obsolete. With the passing of time, original forests and landmarks and other clues to the place name may have disappeared. With a shrug, locals will often say, 'I dunno, it was always called something like that, but no one really knows what it meant.' So now it's our turn to build and rebuild, to name and rename.

I have no love for motorway or junction numbers. The N4 will always be the Sligo Road to me. As for Junction 6 on the M8, well, that will always be 'Horse and Jockey'. Indeed, ye olde inns have given us some of our most colourful place names, like Newtwopothouse near Mallow in County Cork. We also have the place name 'Fox and Geese' in Counties Clare and Dublin. 'Robinhood' was once a popular public-house name in Ireland, and it has left its mark on the map. There's one recorded in 1659 in Dublin near Drimnagh and Robinhood is still the name there to this day. In 1837, there was another Robinhood Inn at Cloonlish in County Roscommon. The area is still referred to as Robinhood. As crass as the name Barack Obama Plaza might seem to some, at least it still tells a story of our time, a story J14 never will.

- - - - - - - - - -
DRIMNAGH
Drimnagh – Droimeanach
Droim – Ridge
Eanach – Marsh
Drimnagh therefore means 'ridge in the marsh'.

- - - - - - - - - -
CLOONLISH
Cloonlish – Cluain Lis
Cluain – Meadow
Lios (Lis) – Ring fort
Cloonlish therefore means 'meadow of the fort'.

We have many fine examples of new place names in both English and Irish. I was sorry to see a place we always knew as 'the daffodil field' in Ballincollig sold for development. Every spring, the entire field would light up as if to say, 'Spring has sprung!' Many years later I had cause to pass the area and, sure enough, there are now houses where the field used to be. As I passed the entrance, my heart lifted as though I had seen a host of golden daffodils. The name at the entrance read 'Daffodil Fields', and the flower of choice blooming in the front gardens was the good old 'daff'.

During the Celtic Tiger years, aspirational names like Bel-Air Heights were in vogue. With respect to the residents, I had little time for such affectation. However, I've come to realise that these names have also recorded the culture of their time, like all good place names should! These names proclaim wealth and ambition, like the Georgian place names of old. Going forward, I feel we should be mindful of our existing *logainmneacha* and what they tell us. A few years ago, on the back road to Waterford, I became stuck in a traffic jam due to flooding up ahead. Outside Mogeely in East Cork, we came to a standstill. I reached into the glovebox for my trusty *foclóir* and set about cracking the code. Yep, it translated as 'the flooded plain'!

MOGEELY

Mogeely – Maigh Dhíle

Maigh – Plain

Díle (Dhíle) – Flood

Mogeely therefore means 'plain of the flood'.

One of the greatest problems with land is that everyone needs some, yet they're not making any more of it. A history of conquest and reconquest is not unique to Ireland. Most countries have seen their borders shift and their place names disappear and sometimes reappear. I remember reading an interview conducted with a representative of the Lenape, the Native American tribe, that once prevailed along the Delaware watershed. They controlled the countryside of modern-day New York, western Long Island, New Jersey and the lower Hudson Valley. Like many of the tribes along America's east coast, they spoke the Algonquian language. The Lenape reportedly sold Manhattan to Dutch settlers for $24 worth of trinkets.

When the reporter asked, 'What did your people call Manhattan before the settlers arrived?'

His monosyllabic answer said it all.

'Ours.'

An unexpected visitor is an unwelcome visitor, and we've had our share of 'cold-callers' over the centuries. The *Dindsenchas* tells us of the Milesians' arrival in Ireland, and history records the arrival of the Viking, Norman and 'New English'. We've had smaller groups like the Huguenot, Palatine, Jew and, in more recent years, groups from Vietnam, Nigeria, Ivory Coast, Poland, Russia and virtually every country on the planet.

I grew up in the very centre of Cork City, where Coburg Street and Devonshire Street meet. The nearby streets are still a treasury of British rule, a who's who and what's what of the British Empire. Apart from Coburg and Devonshire both being celebrated in my actual address, we also had Wellington Road, Waterloo Terrace, Windsor Cottages, Trafalgar Terrace, Marlboro Street, Pembroke Street and many more. The story of Ireland is written in her place names, and so I would hate to think that an entire chapter, albeit a sad one for many, would be erased from 'the book of us'. It's important that future children should ask, 'Why is our address Victoria Terrace? Who was she?'

As recently as this year, there have been calls to replace these street names with the names of Irish patriots. I can fully understand the emotional charge behind such a campaign, but my own feeling is 'let it be'. Let those street signs stand as a reminder to future generations that independence and freedom is not a given. Let them stand as part of the living culture of those amongst us who are descended from the British occupiers. The ones who stayed on.

I'm thinking of the British soldiers and civil servants, like Larcom, the man behind our great place-names survey. Those who developed a *grá* for Ireland. Those who married and settled here and bought in to the idea of an independent Ireland. The folk who clung to Irish shores as the tide receded back to Britain. I'm talking about the Cambridge brothers and the Smyths who played hurling with me in the Camp Field beside the barracks. No more than someone named McAuliffe should wish to shed the name of Olaf, who roamed the sea a thousand years ago, should we wish to modernise the ancient pre-Christian names of Ard Mhacha or

Uisneach. Nor, on foot of declining attendance at Mass, should our more secular society rename Croagh Patrick or the thousands of other Christian place names that bejewel the map of Ireland. *Fág é* ('let it be').

Indeed, I would suggest that we continue the tradition of naming from our own time. The wave of 'new Irish' that arrived on these shores to live amongst us should be commemorated, particularly in the places where they live. Perhaps Gort in County Galway might someday boast a Goiás Avenue to mark the hundreds of Brazilians who moved to Gort from Goiás to fill the need for specialist workers in the meat industry. There are many young immigrant couples here who have taken out Irish passports and now educate their children alongside my own grandchildren in the Irish language Gaelscoil. So perhaps, someday, we will see a bungalow named 'An Pholainnín' meaning 'Little Poland', *as Gaeilge*. It's now our time to write our chapter in the place-names book of Ireland. What about a 'Manila Park' named to honour Filipino nurses and the sacrifice made by frontline workers in the pandemic of 2020, or a playground that acknowledges the wave of African-born Irish children who played there? *Ní neart go cur le chéile* ('there's no strength without unity').

By drilling down into our *logainmneacha*, we release myths and legends, fairies, ancestors and, above all else, a love of place. Like love itself, I believe love of place is not exclusive. If you truly love your own place you will feel the joy of all place. A Kosovan refugee named Armina cut my hair for a number of years when she moved to Ireland. I would often ask her about her home, and she loved to talk about it. She bemoaned the atrocities committed by all sides in the war, and said that she, her boyfriend and her Irish-born baby planned to go home as soon as it was safe again.

In February 2008, I was watching the *Six One News* at home as the new red national flag of Kosovo was unfurled for the first time over Pristina. The post-war economy was in shreds, and the budget for an extravagant public celebration was non-existent. So there would be no military parade or fly-past. However, the people of this tiny republic celebrated their partial UN recognition by baking the biggest chocolate cake in the world. That was that. I hopped up and belted to a filling station for a bunch of red flowers and a modest chocolate cake. When I arrived at the barber shop Armina was smiling and crying, and surrounded by her Turkish, Jamaican and Irish friends.

The greatest place name of them all is 'Home'. Everybody deserves one.

GLOSSARY

PLACE-NAME TERMS

A

Abhainn – River

Abhaill (Úll) – Apple / apple tree / round hillock

Aifreann (Aifrinn) – Mass

Aill – Cliff

Áit – Place / a site

Alt – Height

Aonach – Assembly. Can also mean 'fair'.

Ard – High / height

Ardán – Terrace. Can also mean an elevated place or raised stand.

Ascaill – Avenue

Áth (Átha) – Ford

B

Bá – Bay

Bád – Boat

Baile (Bally) – Place of / home of / homestead / settlement / townland/ town

Baile Nua – Newtown

Barr – Top

Beag – Small

Béal (Bel) – Mouth (of) / opening

Bealach – Road / pass

Bearna – Gap / pass

Bel see Béal

Bile – Sacred tree

Binn – Cliff / peak

Bóthairín – Little road / Laneway. Lána is another
   word used for 'lane'

Bóthar – Road

Breac – Speckled

Brugh – Mansion / palace. Can also allude to a
   'mythical palace'

Buaile – A place set aside for tending to livestock,
   usually cows. Often referred to a milking place in
   summer pasture.

Buí – Yellow

Bun – Foot of, or end of, a river

C

Caipín – Cap

Carn – Pile of rocks

Caiseal – Cashel / stone fort

Caisleán – Castle

Caladh – Landing place, harbour / low-lying land
   beside a river

Cam – Crooked / bent / winding

Caoin – Fair / pleasant

Caol – Narrow / slender, often used when
   referencing a marshy stream

Carraig (Carrick) – Rock

Cathair – City

Cé – Quay

Ceann – Head / headland

Ceathrú – Quarterland

Cill – Church

Cillín – Little church (also indicates a children's
  burial site)

Cladach – Shore / beach

Clais – Ravine

Clár – Indication of a level surface, usually a plain

Cliath – Hurdle

Cloch – Stone, stone building

Clochán – Causeway

Clochar – Stony place

Clós – Close

Cluain – Meadow

Cnoc (Knock) – Hill

Cnocán – Hillock

Coill (Coille, Coillidh, Coillte) – Wood

Coillín – Little wood

Coll – Hazel

Com – Hollow

Cumar (Comar) – Confluence, meeting place of two
  or more streams or rivers

Cora – Weir

Corr – Round hill, pointed hill

Cos (Cois) – Foot. Dative form 'cois' can also mean
  'beside'

Crann – Tree

Crann Úll – Apple tree see Abhaill

Creag – Rock, crag

Creagán – Rocky place

Crois – Crossroads / cross

Cruach – Peak

Cuan – Harbour / bay

Cúirt – Court

Cuileann – Holly

Currach (Corrach) – Marsh

D

Daingean – Fortress

Dair – Oak

Dearg – Red

Dá / Dhá – Two

Díseart – Hermitage

Doirín – Little oak wood

Droichead – Bridge

Droim / Dromainn – Ridge

Dubh – Black

Dún – Fort

E

Eaglais – Church

Eanach – Marsh, watery place

F

Fada – Long

Faiche – Green, lawn

Fearann – Land, territory

Feart – Grave-mound

Fiodh – Wood

Fionn – Fair, white

Fuarán (Uarán) – Spring, fountain

Fuinseog (Fuinse, Fuinseann, Uinse) – Ash tree

G

Gabhar – Goat

Gall – Foreigner. Can also mean 'standing stone'

Gaortha – Wooded river valley, river bed

Gaoth – Wind. Can also mean an 'estuary'

Garbh – Rough

Garraí – Garden

Geal – Bright

Gearr (Giorra) – Short

Glas – Green. Can also mean 'grey' or 'stream'

Gleann – Valley / glen

Goirtín – Little field

Gort – Field

Greanach – Sandy or gravelly place

Gualainn (Guala) – Shoulder

I

Inbhear – Mouth of the river / estuary

Inis – Island

Iolar – Eagle

Iúr – Yew tree

K

Kil/Kill *see* Cill

L

Ladhar – Fork

Lag *see* Log

Lathach (Laitheach) – Mud, muddy place

Láithreach – Site / building ruins

Lann – Land, ground; house, church

Leac – Flat stone

Leaca (Leacain, Leacan) – Hillside

Leacht – Monument / grave mound

Léana – Watery meadow

Leath – Half / side

Léim – Leap / jump

Leitir – Hillside

Liag / Lia – Pillar stone

Liath (Léith) – Grey or grey place

Lios – Liss / ring fort / enclosure

Lios an Uisce – Fort of the water

Lisín – Small liss / small ring fort / small enclosure

Loch – Lake or inlet

Log (Lag) – Hollow

M

Maor (M(h)aoir) – Steward

Muir (Mara) – Sea

Muire (Mhuire) – Mary / Marian

Machaire – Flat place / plain

Maigh (Magh, Má) – Plain

Mainistir – Monastery

Maol – Bare or flat topped. Can also mean 'derelict'

Mín – Smooth level land / mountain pasture

Móin (Móna) – Bog / bogland

Móinín – Small bog / small bogland

Mór – Big / large

Muc – Pig

Muileann – Mill

Mullach (Mullaigh, Mhullaigh) – Hilltop

Mullán – Green field / hillock

Nead – Nest

Nua – New

O

Oileán – Island

P

Páirc – Field / park

Place – Plás

Poll – Pool / (tidal) hole / hole

Port – Port / bank

Púca – Pooka / goblin

R

Rae – row (in street names)

Ré – Level place / plain

Radharc – View

Raithneach (Raithean, Raithní, Raithneacha) – Fern, place of ferns

Ráithín – Small fort / small ring fort

Ráth – Fort / ring fort

Rinn – Headland / point in the landscape

Ros – Wood / wooded elevation

Rua (Ruadh) – Red. Can also mean 'a red place'

S

Sagart – Priest

Sail – Willow tree

Saileach – Willow trees (collectively)

Scairt – Shelter / undergrowth / thicket

Sceach (Sceich) – Hawthorn bush. Can also mean 'thorn bush'

Sceichín – A small thorn bush

Sean – Old / ancient

Seascann (Seisceann) – Swampy land, bog

Sí / Sídhe – Fairy. Can also mean 'palace or residence
of the fairies'

Sionnach – Fox

Sliabh – Mountain / moor

Sráid – Street. Can also mean 'village'

Sráidbhaile – Village

Sruth – Stream

T

Tamhlacht – Burial place, usually pagan

Taobh – Hillside

Teach – House / homestead / (of a saint or cleric)
church

Teampall – Church

Theas – South / southern

Thuaidh – North / northern

Tír – Land / territory

Tobar – Well / spring / water source

Tóchar – Causeway

Tóin (Tón) – Bottom, bottomland

Tor – Steep rocky height / bush

Trá – Beach / strand

Trian (Treana) – Third (part of)

Tuama / Tuaim – Gravemound / burial place / tomb

Tuairín – Little field or paddock

Tuar – Paddock or field

Tulach (Tulaigh) – Hillock

U

Uachtar – Upper, southern part

Uachtarach (Uacht) – Upper

Uaimh – Cave

Uinse *see* Fuinseog

Uisce – Water

Úll – *see* abhaill

MY PLACE NAMES

PLACE NAME	LOCATION	NOTES

PLACE NAME	LOCATION	NOTES

PLACE NAME	LOCATION	NOTES

PLACE NAME	LOCATION	NOTES

PLACE NAME   **LOCATION**   **NOTES**

PLACE NAME	LOCATION	NOTES

PLACE NAME	LOCATION	NOTES

PLACE NAME	LOCATION	NOTES

PLACE NAME	LOCATION	NOTES

PLACE NAME	LOCATION	NOTES

PLACE NAME	LOCATION	NOTES

PLACE NAME	LOCATION	NOTES

PLACE NAME	LOCATION	NOTES

PLACE NAME	LOCATION	NOTES

PLACE NAME	LOCATION	NOTES

PLACE NAME	LOCATION	NOTES

PLACE NAME	LOCATION	NOTES

PLACE NAME	LOCATION	NOTES